THE SEVEN CITIES
OF CÍBOLA

THE
SEVEN CITIES
OF CÍBOLA

BY
STEPHEN CLISSOLD

Clarkson N. Potter, Inc./Publisher

NEW YORK

This edition first published 1962
© 1961 Stephen Clissold
Printed in Great Britain

Contents

ENDPAPERS

Illustrations

PLATES

ACKNOWLEDGMENTS

Acknowledgment is gratefully made to the Trustees of the British Museum for permission to reproduce the engravings of Theodore de Bry, the illustrations from Herrera's *Historia General* and Harrisse's *Discovery of North America*, and the maps of Johannes Ruysch and Johannes Martines. Acknowledgment is also due to the Rare Book Division of New York Public Library for the sketch of a buffalo, and to the U.S. Information Service for the photographs of the Indian Pueblos.

The Spanyards have notice of Seven Cities which old men of the Indians show them should lie towards the north-east from Mexico. They have used and use daily much diligence in seeking of them, but they cannot find any one of them. They say that the witchcraft of the Indians is such that when they come by these townes they cast a mist upon them so that they cannot see them.

From Hakluyt's *Principal Navigations*.

CHAPTER I

Columbus

Before the end of the first day of 1492, it was clear that Spain had reached its year of destiny. For months past, King Ferdinand of Aragón and Queen Isabel of Castille had been mustering their forces for an assault on the last Islamic stronghold remaining in Spain. The Moorish armies which, seven and a half centuries before, had swept up from Africa, submerging the Iberian peninsula and even threatening to overrun France, had been gradually pushed back; small militant Christian Kingdoms had been established – Navarre, León-Castille, Aragón, Portugal. These states had been gradually welded together by treaty, purchase or dynastic marriage, until now, except for Portugal, they stood united in arms under Ferdinand and Isabel, the Catholic Sovereigns, and poised for the final thrust.

All that remained under the Crescent, in this last decade of the fifteenth century, was the small Kingdom of Granada, splendid in its setting of wild mountain and smiling vega, and still formidable despite its isolation. Its massive walls and towers shielded a population of two hundred thousand souls. From time to time, richly accoutred horsemen would sally out to provoke the besiegers to single combat, and the Christian Knights were not slow to take up the challenge. But the war was more than a picturesque affair of mediaeval jousting. Inexorably, the Catholic Sovereigns pressed on for final victory. In the middle of the previous summer, the Christian camp had been thrown into confusion when the hangings of a pavilion caught fire and a large part of the Spaniards' baggage and treasure was burnt. But this misfortune was turned into a shrewd stroke of psychological warfare. To safeguard the camp against such disasters in the future and to demonstrate the will of the Christians to invest Granada until it should fall, the Sovereigns resolved that a permanent city should take the place of the encampment of tents. Troops from the different regions of Spain were given the task of building their own quarters, and within a matter of weeks a redoubtable new settlement – part fortified camp and part city, with well laid out streets and houses of stone and mortar and with stabling for a thousand horses, confronted the dismayed people of Granada. With its stark, rectangular ground-plan, its massive portals, its spacious central plaza, it still stands today – the prototype of countless cities founded by the men whose conquering zeal was to carry them to the new lands discovered that same year beyond the Atlantic Ocean.

In the closing months of 1491, negotiations were conducted for the surrender of Granada to the Christians. The talks took place in deep secrecy, now in a small hamlet outside the city, now behind the walls of the Moorish capital itself. At the end of November, terms were finally agreed. Granada was to be surrendered, with due safeguards for the lives, liberties, and properties of the inhabitants, within two months. But news of the impending capitulation leaked out, causing fierce resentment amongst the more fanatical Moslems. Boabdil, the last King of Granada, feared for his own safety and hurriedly advanced the date of the surrender to 2 January.

On the morning of that day, with the ceremonies befitting the closing of a phase of history which had lasted more than seven centuries, the Grand Cardinal Mendoza rode out at the head of the Spanish *corps d'élite* to take formal possession of the Alhambra, the residence of the Moorish Kings. Ferdinand, with a magnificent entourage of courtiers and nobles, waited outside the city walls to receive Boabdil's submission. Boabdil surrendered the keys of the Alhambra with the words: 'These are thine, oh King, since such is the will of Allah; use thy victory with mercy and moderation.' He then rode on to make similar obeisance to Queen Isabel, before setting out for the small principality which had been assigned to him in the barren Alpujarras under the terms of the capitulation. At a hill where the path turned away from the fertile vega below, and which is still traditionally known as El Sospiro del Moro, Boabdil turned to look for the last time on his abandoned capital. 'You do well to weep like a woman,' his mother is reported to have rebuked him, 'for what you failed to defend like a man.'[1] Ferdinand and Isabel, too, stood gazing across the vale towards Granada until they could see, glittering in the winter sunshine, the great silver cross which Ferdinand had borne with him through the campaign and the banners of the Christian army raised above the city walls. Then they moved forward to take solemn possession of this last fragment of Moorish territory. The epic of the Reconquista – the long reconquest of Spain from Islam – was over; the epic of the Conquista – the winning of a new continent beyond the sea – was soon to begin.

The man who was to link together these two historical processes was a witness of that scene. His origins were obscure; he was a stranger known to his contemporaries as Cristóbal Colón and later, to the English-speaking world, as Christopher Columbus. 'I saw the royal banners of Your Highnesses on the towers of the Alhambra,' he wrote later to the Sovereigns, 'and I watched the Moorish King come out to the city gates and kiss your royal hands.' It must have been a moment of deep emotion for him. He saw history as one great crusade, with himself destined to play a leading part in it. The fall of Granada (some consolation, though a modest one, for the loss of Constantinople forty years before) brought nearer the time when the infidel hordes would be rolled back from the sacred places of Christendom. The discoveries of new lands in the west, which he was

[1] Quoted by Prescott, *History of the Reign of Ferdinand and Isabella.* Vol. 1, p. 481.

15

confident God had reserved for him, would yield resources for the final winning of the Holy Sepulchre.

In the mind of this extraordinary man, mystic visions did not exclude the most practical of calculations. The fall of Granada, he hoped, would give a decisive turn for the better to his own personal fortunes. The royal Commission, which for five years had been deliberating his projects for reaching the East by sailing westward across the uncharted ocean, had finally pronounced them impossible. The Sovereigns had accepted the Commission's findings, but the Queen had spoken consoling words to the petitioner and promised that, once her mind was free of preoccupations with the war against the Moors, she would hear him again. Isabel was as good as her word. As soon as Granada had fallen, the Commission was instructed to give Columbus's proposals fresh consideration. But once again, before the end of January, it reported adversely. Columbus, rebuffed but not crushed, left Santa Fé determined to carry his proposals to the French court; but before he had travelled two leagues, he was overtaken by a royal messenger and summoned to return. The Queen had decided to accept his proposals and grant his demands in full. This sudden change of mind is not easy to explain. Perhaps the previous rejection was no more than bluff, practised in the hope that the foreign adventurer would moderate his unheard-of demands for honours, rights and privileges. Or it may be that the Queen had received fresh evidence which lent colour to Columbus's ideas and indicated that some other monarch was ready to back them. Or it may be that Isabel simply let herself be persuaded by the last minute intercession of men like Santangel, the astute Jewish converso and financier, who gave powerful support to Columbus and offered to provide funds to support his enterprise. Whatever the explanation may be, Columbus was informed that his proposals were accepted. After some weeks of drafting and discussion, a formal agreement was drawn up and signed.

On 2 August, 1492, a fleet of three small ships – the *Santa María*, the *Pinta*, and the *Niña* – furnished by the port of Palos and manned by crews recruited mainly by the Pinzons, a family of respected local mariners, set out on their voyage of discovery.

Columbus made first for the Canary Islands, then set a westerly course into the unknown. The charts which he had with him marked the legendary islands of St Brandon and Antillia but, though he kept a sharp look-out for them, he found nothing; and it was only on 12 October, ten weeks after leaving Palos, that Columbus made landfall. He had reached the Bahamas. He then coasted along from island to island, and touched the coasts of Cuba and Haiti, which he named Española (Hispaniola). There the *Santa María* foundered, and her timbers were used for the building of a settlement, Navidad, where Columbus left a small garrison before setting a homeward course for Spain.

In the report which he sent to the Sovereigns, the Admiral extolled the exotic beauty of the islands he had discovered, with their 'hills and mountains, vales and meadows, land so fair and rich for planting and sowing, and for breeding every sort of cattle, for building towns and villages . . . as much gold as Their Highnesses may need, spice and cotton at their command . . . and a thousand precious things.' And if there should be any in Spain to doubt his words, they had but to look upon the nuggets of gold, the samples of spices, and the copper-skinned inhabitants themselves, which he had brought back with him. The Sovereigns accorded to him a magnificent reception at court, and confirmed him in his titles, honours, and privileges. The news of his discoveries spread through Spain, while versions of his Report, in Latin and other languages, and the correspondence of scholars spread knowledge of them throughout Europe.

But what exactly had the Admiral discovered? The court seems at first to have accepted his claim that he had reached 'The Indies' – i.e. India, China, and the countries of the Far

East (whose inhabitants became therefore 'Indians') – but there were scholars such as Peter Martyr of Anghiera, the Italian humanist who had settled in Spain, who held from the outset that the size of the globe was so great that this must be ruled out. Columbus himself claims in his Report that he had found a coast (that of Cuba) 'so long that I deemed it to be the mainland – the province of Cathay' (China).

In authorizing the Admiral to undertake a second voyage, the Sovereigns instructed him to continue the exploration of this coast and to discover whether or not the interior led to the cities and rich trading centres of China. The Admiral was, in any case, to establish suitable trading posts in the lands discovered, and – since the crusading zeal of the Reconquista still moved men's minds – he was enjoined, above all, to see to the conversion of the natives to the Christian faith.

Whatever the new lands might prove to be, there was now no lack of adventurers eager to enlist and seek their fortunes under the Admiral. At Cadiz an impressive fleet of seventeen vessels was assembled, carrying more than twelve hundred soldiers, sailors, officials, and colonists, together with a quantity of seeds and agricultural tools, and the first horses, cattle, and swine to be introduced into the New World. The fleet sailed on 25 September, 1493, and after a fair voyage reached the Lesser Antilles, whose fertility and genial charm contrasted strikingly with the ferocity of their inhabitants – the cannibal Caribs. After visiting a number of islands, including a large one which a shipmate of the Admiral, Juan Ponce de León, was later to subdue and which we know as Puerto Rico, Columbus reached Española. Here tragic news awaited him. The small garrison had clashed with the natives and been wiped out. The first attempt at settlement in the New World had ended in disaster.

The Admiral then chose a fresh site, established what he intended to be a trading post and sent an expedition into the interior to search for more gold. Some was indeed found, to his great delight, and sent back to Spain. But, even with this encouragement, the colony began to falter. The site proved unhealthy, most of the livestock died, and food was short. The Indians, whose curiosity had turned to fear, possessed little that they could barter. Hidalgos and soldiers of fortune, who deemed it dishonourable to toil with their hands, were compelled to share in the menial tasks by which the settlement just managed to keep alive. The Admiral himself sailed off on a five months' voyage of exploration during which he discovered Jamaica, and then reconnoitred the south coast of Cuba.

These discoveries still did not help Columbus to solve the problem of whether he had reached the Far East, although he made his shipmates take oath that the coast of Cuba was really part of a continent. No wishful thinking, however, could obscure the gravity of the situation which confronted him when he returned to his colony, by which time he himself had fallen gravely ill. The early relationship of tolerant friendliness between the settlers and the natives had turned to arrogance, impatience, and callous exploitation on the side of the Spaniards, and to terror and hopelessness on that of the Indians. After further ruthless attempts to wrest from the natives their last grains of gold – the precious metal Columbus extolled, with almost mystical fervour, as 'most excellent; of gold is treasure made; the man who possessed gold does all that he desires in the world, and can even send souls to Paradise' – the Admiral sailed once more for Spain.

The spoils which Columbus had brought back with him was sufficient to earn the thanks of the Sovereigns and their permission to fit out a third expedition. The lands discovered he now declared to be the Ophir of King Solomon, and paraded the natives, with their feather headdresses and barbaric ornaments, to bolster his claim. But the famished, fever-stricken, and resentful colonists who had returned with him had a very different story to tell. The golden hopes which had brought men flocking to enlist in their hundreds had now faded. As a spur to recruitment, criminals serving prison sentences were offered pardons if they would embark. Even so, more than a year passed before funds could be raised, three hundred volunteers enrolled, and a fleet of six ships dispatched.

It is possible that the Sovereigns may only have thought it worthwhile to back the Admiral's third voyage (1498-1500) when they learned that the King of Portugal had certain knowledge of the existence of a continent behind the screen of Columbus's islands and that he was fitting out a strong expedition, probably under Vasco da Gama, to take possession of it. The Admiral, resolved on fresh and still greater discoveries, set a more southerly course across the Atlantic than before, and at length sighted and christened the island of Trinidad, and navigated the fearful straits, which he named Serpent's Mouth and Dragon's Mouth, where the Orinoco River pours into the sea. Water in such volume clearly could only be drained from a great continent. Was this the land, then, that the King of Portugal was seeking? Was this, indubitably at last, the mainland of Asia? 'I believe that this is a very great continent,' Columbus recorded in his Journal, 'until today unknown.' Elsewhere he refers to it as 'another world'. Brooding on the mystery, bolstering the evidence of his shrewd mariner's eyes with tags culled from his reading of the Bible and works of doubtful geographic lore, he concluded that he had come upon no less a spot than the Terrestrial Paradise, 'the end of the East', perched, moreover – according to a still more remarkable flight of fancy – on a protuberance on the globe, like the nipple of a woman's breast. Pearls adorned the approaches to this Paradise – pearls in unbelievable profusion – offered by the natives from the rich pearl-fisheries of Paria.

Meanwhile, events in Española were making that colony

the reverse of paradise. Bartholomew and Diego, his brothers to whom the Admiral had delegated authority in his absence, had proved feeble administrators. Discontent blazed into open mutiny. So shrill and clamant were the complaints voiced at Court against the Admiral and his brothers, that the King appointed a royal commissioner, Bobadilla, to go out to Española with the fullest powers. Soon after his arrival, Bobadilla stripped the three Columbus brothers of office and sent them back to Spain in chains. To the proud and sensitive man who knew that he had won a new empire for Spain, it was an hour of darkest humiliation and injustice; and the bitterness remained, even after the Sovereigns had received him with words of solace and reassurance. Though commissioned by them to undertake a fourth voyage, he was not reinstated in his viceregal powers. Other adventurers too, disregarding the monopoly accorded him in the original capitulations, were beginning to make voyages of exploration of their own, and to found settlements throughout the islands and the adjoining mainland.

But these other voyages had done little more to solve the puzzle of the lands which Christopher Columbus had first discovered. Was this the coast of Asia, and if so, how did it lie in relation to the cities of the Great Khan, India, and the other parts of the Far East where the Portuguese had already established their trading posts? If Cuba was indeed a province of the Chinese mainland, as Columbus held it to be (though at times he claimed it was Cipango or Japan), while to the South lay the land-mass of the Terrestrial Paradise, must there not be a sea passage between the two – a strait that led to the Indian Ocean and would serve as the quickest route from Europe to the rich trading centres of the Orient? Here, before the nature of the American continent was understood or the existence of the Pacific Ocean suspected, is a foreshadowing of that Search for the Straits which was to become an obsession with explorers until Magellan, in 1520, came upon it at the southern tip of the continent. Thereafter their goal became the Northern, or North-west, Passage.

The Admiral set out on his fourth and final voyage to the Indies in May 1502, in the hope that this time he could complete the pattern of his earlier discoveries. He had been given strict orders not to call at Española, for the Sovereigns feared he would clash with Bobadilla, the Governor they had appointed to succeed him. Miraculously escaping a hurricane which destroyed twenty out of the thirty ships which were sailing from Española to Spain loaded with treasure and passengers, of whom Bobadilla was one, Columbus crossed the Caribbean and reached what is now the coast of Honduras. Here he was faced with an important decision. The coast of the mainland, at this point, ran east and west – which direction should he take? Columbus chose to set course to the east. Had he turned instead to the west, his route would have led along the Gulf of Mexico to the domains, not of the Great Khan, but of Montezuma. Already, before striking the coast of Honduras, he had missed a clue which fate had let fall across his path – a large canoe of a size and design hitherto unknown to the Spaniards. It was bound on a trading expedition to the neighbouring islands and carried a cargo of finely woven garments, sheets of dyed cotton and implements of cotton which the Indians declared they had brought from the west. But the Admiral had thoughts only for the Straits which he believed he would find by keeping a course to the east. The canoe passed on – it was left to other pioneers to retrace its course and to sail round the bulging land-mass of Yucatan, to the realm of Montezuma.

Columbus kept to his course, against adverse winds and currents, until he rounded the point which he thankfully christened Cape Gracias a Díos, and veered south to explore the coasts of Nicaragua, Costa Rica and the Isthmus of Panama. From the natives the Admiral gleaned hints, half understood and coloured by his own conjectures, of a rich land lying but a few days' journey inland. It was washed by the sea, they gave him to understand – the same sea, he assumed, as that on which he was sailing – and he pressed on impatient to double the Cape and enter the Straits which should lead to this new land. But the search was fruitless. At length, the Admiral reached a point to which other explorers, sailing from the opposite direction, had come. There was nothing for it now but to turn back.

An attempt to establish a settlement on the mainland ended in failure. Then, after further hazards and hardships, including being stranded for a year on the coast of Jamaica, Columbus returned to Española and from there, in 1504, to Spain, where two years later he died. Immense though his achievements had been, his vaster, more fantastic dreams remained unrealized. The holy places of Christendom still lay in the hands of the infidels. The Admiral directed in his will that part of the wealth accruing to him from the Indies should be devoted to their redemption, and enjoined his heirs to undertake this solemn task on his behalf.

'Seek and ye shall find' – no man had sought with more heroic and inspired constancy than Columbus, and none had found so abundantly. But whether he had found what he had sought, or whether it was something entirely different – that remained a tormenting uncertainty. In moments of exaltation he would claim that he had not only reached the mainland of Asia, but lands of travellers' tales and of classical and biblical lore as well. 'This island,' he wrote of Española, 'is Tarsis, is Scythia, is Ophir, and Ophaz, and Cipango.' His son Fernando, in his biography of the Admiral, adds that it was also Antillia. Peter Martyr, who kept the scholars of Europe informed of the wonders of the New World in his voluminous correspondence, shared his view. 'If we consider the description given by the cosmographers,' he wrote, 'it seems that both these and other islands adjoining are the isles of Antillia.'

CHAPTER II

Antillia, Seven Cities and a Fountain

On most of the charts produced before Columbus's discoveries, and even for some time after, a number of islands of varying size were marked as lying far out in the Atlantic Ocean: St Brandon, the magic isle of the Irish Saints; others, south of Cape Verde, 'which were held to be floating on the surface of the water'; and yet others, Fernando Columbus says, 'that burn perpetually'. Most important of all was that island which Peter Martyr and Fernando Columbus believed Española to be, and which the Florentine cosmographer Toscanelli had mentioned to Columbus in a famous letter – 'the Island of Antillia, called of the Seven Cities, of which you know'.

Martin Behaim's map of the world clearly indicates both St Brandon and Antillia, the latter some thirty degrees west of Madeira and twenty-five south-west of the Azores, and it gives an explanation of the legendary Seven Cities that were to be found on Antillia. 'In the year of Christ 734, when the whole of Spain had been won by the heathen of Africa, the above island called Seven Cities was settled by an Archbishop from Opporto in Portugal, with six other bishops, and other Christians, men and women, who had fled thither from Spain by ship, together with their cattle, belongings, and goods. In 1414 a ship from Spain got very close to it without being endangered.'[1]

Fernando Columbus gives a fuller version of the same story.[2] The Carthaginians, he asserts, were said by the

[1] See also map of Johann Ruysch (c. 1508), reproduced opposite page 48.
[2] *La historia della vita e dei Fatti di Cristofero Colombo*, Chapter IX.

24

ancients to have discovered, but not colonized it. Then in 714 A.D., when Don Rodrigo of Spain lost his kingdom to the Moors, 'they say there took ship seven Bishops, and with their people and ships went to that island where each of them built a city; and lest their people should think to return to Spain, they set fire to their ships and all their rigging and other things necessary for navigation. And some Portuguese say of this island that many Portuguese came to it and never returned again.' Once, Don Fernando goes on to relate, in the time of Prince Henry the Navigator, a band of Portuguese was begged to stay and meet the ruler of the island, but fearing they would be detained, the sailors took fright and sailed away. Prince Henry was very angry when he heard this, and ordered them to return forthwith to the island. But the Captain and his crew were still alarmed and sailed away from Portugal without daring to follow the Prince's commands, despite the fact that some of the men had found on their previous voyage that a third part of the sand they had scooped up from the shore for scouring the galley pots and pans, turned out to be grains of the purest gold!

Antillia – 'Ante-ilha', the island out opposite, the island in front – was still believed to exist by the Portuguese in the fifteenth century, and a number of attempts (which, if pursued a little further, might well have anticipated the discoveries of Columbus) were made by them to reach it. Around the middle of the century, Diego de Teive, who discovered Flores, the most isolated of the Azores, set off in quest of it with his pilot Pedro de Velasco. They gave up the search after sailing some 120 sea-miles to the west. Teive later conceded his claims in Flores, and with them his rights to explore, to another Portuguese, Fernao Telles. In 1475 the Portuguese Crown renewed these privileges, specifically conferring on Telles the right to discover Antillia. Whether Telles ever ventured out on the quest is not known, and two years later he was dead.

Similar obscurity conceals the movements of the man who succeeded to Telles' rights of exploration. This was a mariner of Flemish extraction, known to the Portuguese as Fernam Dulmo, who had settled in the Azores. On 3 March, 1485 (the very year that the Portuguese Crown rejected the proposals put forward by Columbus for the sponsorship of a western voyage), conferred on Dulmo the rights to 'a large island, islands, or mainland, beyond our shores, presumed to be the island of the Seven Cities'. Dulmo seems to have found difficulty in raising the funds and securing the ships for this expedition to Antillia, and took into partnership Estreito, a rich man of Madeira, who was to receive half the islands or lands discovered. The expedition was to consist of two ships, one commanded by Dulmo, who would set the course for the first forty days, and the other by his partner Estreito, who should take over the command if Antillia had not by then been discovered. The documents also refer to the participation in the expedition of an unnamed German, in all probability Martin Behaim, who had marked the position of Antillia on his map. The expedition was to have set out in March 1487, but by June it was still delayed in Terceira. Did it in fact ever sail? No more is heard of Dulmo and his quest. But Antillia, though never found, was not forgotten. Its name lives on in the designation given to the islands of the Greater and the Lesser Antilles, and the legend of its Seven Cities, seeping down through popular memory, re-emerges unexpectedly, far removed in space and time and with fresh and vigorous impetus, in the lands of the New World.

The Indians of the New World also had their lore of strange and fabulous islands. The natives of Haiti and Cuba believed, according to Oviedo, Herrera, and other chroniclers, in the existence of a magic spring or river which had the power to restore youth to those who drank of it or bathed in its waters. This spring was reputed to be on an island variously referred to as Ananeo, Boyuca, or (more frequently) Bimini. Bimini was believed to lie 'at a distance of three hundred and twenty-five leagues from Española'.[1] This story spread quickly amongst the credulous Spanish adventurers, and even won a certain credence at Court. Peter Martyr gives it frequent and serious attention. 'Do not think, Your Highness,' he wrote in December 1514, 'that they say this lightly or in jest. So seriously have they dared tell this throughout the Court that all the people, and not a few of those whom virtue and fortune distinguish from the populace, hold it to be true. But if Your Highness asks my opinion,' the cautious scholar adds, 'I will tell you that I cannot concede such power to Mother Nature, and I believe that God has reserved this prerogative for himself.'

But tales of the Fountain of Youth continued to circulate, and Peter Martyr returned to the theme a few years later, in describing the expedition made in 1520 to the coast of what is now Carolina, by a lawyer named Lucas Vasquez de Ayllón. The latter, as also the Licentiate Figueroa, President of the Audiencia in Española, and another gentleman of high repute, 'unanimously declare that they have heard of the Fountain which restores vigour, and attach some credence to those who told about it', though they had not had the luck to find it themselves. They were particularly impressed by the story of a native servant called Andreas the Bearded, who maintained that his father had found the magic fountain when he was a very old man – such was its potency that he returned home rejuvenated, took a young wife, and begat a son. Could such a phenomenon, seemingly contrary to the laws of nature, be believed? Peter Martyr marshalled the evidence of classical mythology and natural history – the rejuvenating potions of Medea, the enchantments of Circe, and nature's power to slough off the skins of snakes, with a wealth of other dubious instances – and sagely concluded that 'I

[1] Peter Martyr: *Decadas del Nuevo Mundo*; Decada 2, Libro 10, cap. 2.

would not be surprised that the waters of the Fountain so sought after may have some aqueous or aereous quality unknown to us, of moderating the melancholy [of old age] by restoring strength'. The Indians of the New World – and if Indians, why not Spaniards too? – might thus seek out the health-giving waters 'in the same way as our people go from Rome to the baths of Puteoli in Naples to recover their health'.[1]

But if, in the mind of a humanist at Court, the Fountain of Bimini might seem really little more than a sort of Indian spa, the ardent imagination of a conquistador would accept such stories in their most literal and spectacular form. He would be concerned not with discussing, but with finding it; and while Peter Martyr was speculating about the possibility of the Fountain's existence, the first expedition had in fact already set out in search of it.

The moving spirit in this enterprise was Juan Ponce de León – 'a Captain, a good man, and a gentleman', says the chronicler Oviedo, who knew him well. The object of the quest must have appealed strongly to him, for Ponce de León was now getting on in years. He had come out to the Indies with Columbus on his second voyage, and played an active part, with his ferocious war-dog Becerillo, in the subjugation of Española. Then, in 1508, he had undertaken the conquest of the neighbouring island of Puerto Rico but the governorship was taken from him in the contest for authority which followed the death of Christopher Columbus. Although he could still have lived comfortably on the produce of his land and his mines, yet – Oviedo puts it – 'he could not rest content where others commanded'. He therefore equipped a fresh expedition in the hope that thereby 'he would, serving God and King, double or increase his wealth, augment his person with titles of honour and state', at the same time 'seeking to renovate, rejuvenate, and refresh his age and vigour, as one who drank or bathed

[1] Peter Martyr: *Decadas del Nuevo Mundo*; Decada 7, Libro 7, cap. 1.

in that famous fountain should'.[1] On his petition, the Crown granted him the right to discover the island of 'Beniny' (Bimini) and to be its Adelantado or Governor.

Other adventurers from the islands had probably made unauthorized probes to the north before Ponce de León left with his expedition in 1512. A map published in Seville the previous year marks a vague land mass to the north of Cuba 'region of the Isle of Bemini', and a note on the reverse states: 'To the north, there have been discovered marvellous countries and lands.' But if other Spaniards had forestalled Ponce de León in quest of slaves, gold and fame, the life-giving Fountain had eluded them and the records bear no trace of their names.

For this expedition, Ponce de León secured two ships and the services of a veteran pilot called Antón de Alaminos. After skirting the chain of the Bahamas, they fell in with another roving vessel, and on Easter Day sighted land – whether island or mainland they could not tell – which they christened La Florida, after the Spanish name for Easter (Pascua Florida) and also 'since it must have appeared fair and luxuriant'.[2]

Ponce de León's landfall must have been on the east coast of the peninsula, somewhere near the mouth of St John's River. The natives showed no sign of fear, but loosed off their arrows against the strangers. It seemed they had met with Spaniards before, for one old Indian shouted out a few words of Spanish. But of the Fountain of Youth they clearly neither knew nor cared anything at all.

The expedition turned south, making heavy going against the flow of the Gulf Stream, and rounded the southern tip of the peninsula. The shore was everywhere low and swampy, with no promise of good harbours. Leaving Alaminos, with two Indian guides, to explore the shoals, Ponce de León decided to turn back. Three weeks later he

[1] Oviedo, *Historia General y natural de las Indias*, parte 2, Libro 36, cap. 1.
[2] Las Casas, *Historia de las Indias*, Libro 3, cap. 20, Tomo 2, p. 144.

was safe in Puerto Rico where Alaminos later joined him. 'Having found Bimini but not the Fountain,' records Herrera, summing up the results of the expedition, 'the other ship arrived with the report that it was a large island with many streams and groves.'[1] From now on, men were to speak of the 'island' as La Florida: the vision of Bimini and its magic fountain slowly faded, and the name survives today to denote only two tiny islands lying about fifty miles off the coast east of Miami.

In the years that followed Ponce de León was kept from his dreams of conquest and colonization by the necessity of warring against the Caribs. But the hope of returning to La Florida never left him. 'He realized,' Oviedo writes, 'that he had been hoaxed and misled; but undaunted by past experience and hardship, he once again, with more discretion and at greater cost, fitted out a fleet. . . . It seemed to him that as well as what could be discovered about the islands in those parts, many important and secret things could be learned on the mainland, and those people could be converted to God with great benefit to himself and to those who accompanied him, who were two hundred men, with fifty horses.'

The south-west coast of Florida, where Ponce de León made his second attempt to establish a colony, was inhabited by the Calusa, a tribe believed to be of Carib origin who settled in the peninsula many centuries before the coming of the Spaniards. They were a hardy and warlike people, who drew a frugal sustenance from fish and oyster beds and had been known to travel in their canoes as far as Cuba and Española. Like the other tribes of Florida, the Calusa were formidable bowmen who fiercely opposed all intruders.

The country was as little suited to colonization as the character of the natives who inhabited it. The low, gentle coastline, wafting its fragrance across the waters, proved on closer inspection to be an endless tangled fringe of

[1] *Historia General*, Decada 1, Libro 9, cap. 11, Tomo 2, pp. 211-12.

mangrove-covered islets, half submerged by swift-flowing tidal currents. The tip of the peninsula curved round to enclose a bay which still bears the name of Ponce de León. Behind it, in the area now known as the Everglades, stretched a flooded waste of sawgrass studded with cypress hammocks and clumps of palm. Nor was the east coast any more inviting as the Spaniards had already discovered, since the approaches were rendered perilous because of the long ribbon of sand bars, on which the great tourist towns of today now stand. Florida was a land of myriad lakes, ranging from vast inland seas like Okeechobee, to shallow, stagnant pools into which the Indian braves would plunge at need and discharge their arrows from behind some half submerged log. Half way down the west coast of the peninsula, the deep inlet of Tampa Bay, which the Spaniards christened Bahía del Espíritu Santo, promised easier access to the interior. Beyond it rose a back-bone of rolling land, pitted with lakes and springs and variegated with stretches of prairie and patches of pine and palmetto, stretching for half the length of the peninsula. But if the explorer continued northwards from Tampa along the coast, he would meet only with the same maze of slough and island until, at Apalachee Bay, the coast began to curve round westwards towards the delta of the Mississippi.

Where, in this fertile yet inhospitable land, could Ponce de León hope to gain a footing for his soldiers and colonists? The requirements for a settlement were easy to define but hard to discover; a safe anchorage for his ships, a stretch of level ground where a fortified camp could be built and sufficient land held in safety for the crops and livestock necessary for its maintenance; or, if the natives remained hostile, a terrain where they could be brought to combat and feel the full effect of the Spaniards' firearms and cavalry. But the Indians, though invariably hostile, would not let themselves be drawn into pitched battles. They preferred to lurk in ambush in their woods and swamps, picking off the enemy with their deadly shafts when the Spaniards came to draw water or pitch their camp. The Indians were not interested in trade. Worshippers of the sun and moon, they showed no eagerness to learn about the white men's god. They were little impressed by their slow-firing, quickly rusting firearms, or by the mounts which they rode floundering through the swamps.

The exact course of Ponce de León's colonizing fiasco is unknown. We know that he sailed for weeks along the coast searching for a suitable base for settlement and conquest, and meeting everywhere with fierce resistance. In one of these skirmishes, he was severely wounded in the thigh by an arrow. He was obliged to sail back to seek a cure for his wound and the expedition was abandoned. The wound proved fatal and the Govenor died shortly after his return to Puerto Rico. A proud epitaph was engraved upon his tomb: 'Here lies one who was a Lion in Name, still more so in his Deeds.'

Ponce de León's contemporaries were not slow to draw a moral from the fate of the captain who had perished in his quest for the Fountain of Youth. To Friar Bartolomé de las Casas, the converted conquistador who had espoused the cause of the Indians with sacred zeal, the explanation was clear. Ponce de León, like others of his breed, had embarked on his venture with the sole object of adding to his already great wealth and to find fresh Indians 'to molest and tyrannize over'. Disaster had overtaken him 'so that God might reveal the wisdom and justice with which he had made all things and caused all things to be made, that he should undertake an enterprise wherein he might dissipate all he had stolen and piled up over a long period, and finally die an evil death'.[1] The conclusion of Oviedo, an old soldier himself, is equally pious but more charitable. 'It must be believed,' he simply remarks, 'that God did not wish, nor had the time come, for the conversion of that

[1] Las Casas, *Historia de las Indias*, Lib. 3, cap. 20.

R.Hilata

Satirrōa

A pitched battle with the Indians.

The Spaniards celebrate Mass on landing in the New World.

land and province to our Holy Catholic Faith."[1] That time did not come until many years had passed, and much blood of Indians and Spaniards had been shed in the quest for fabled treasure or the surer if less alluring fruits of settlement.

[1] Op. cit.

CHAPTER III

The Narváez Expedition

Nine years had elapsed between Ponce de León's two expeditions to Florida; and it is likely that the second, disastrous venture would never have been undertaken had it not been for the dramatic turn which events had taken in Mexico. For the Spaniards' spectacular triumphs there had given fresh impetus to the whole rhythm of the Conquista.

On Maundy Thursday, 21 April, 1519, Hernán Cortés landed on the island of San Juan de Ulloa in the Gulf of Mexico. He had been commissioned by Diego de Velásquez, the Governor of Cuba, to investigate reports of a rich and powerful state in the hinterland. The following day, Good Friday, he crossed over to the Mexican mainland and pushed into the interior. There his expedition encountered the first wealthy, well organized and semi-civilized community in the New World – the domain of the Aztecs, whose overlord or emperor was Montezuma.

This news, coupled with the tangible evidence of Aztec treasure which soon followed, caused a fever of excitement and expectation throughout the Spanish settlements. Velásquez quickly understood the magnitude of the prize, and realized that Cortés was determined to seize it for himself. He therefore dispatched another officer, Pánfilo de Narváez, with a stronger force to bring Cortés to heel and claim the spoils for the Governor.

Narváez was 'tall and strong-limbed with a red beard and an agreeable presence', writes Bernal Díaz del Castillo, the soldier who fought under Cortés and who, in his old age, wrote a lively history of the whole conquest of Mexico.

'His speech and voice were deep, as though coming from under a vault. He was a good horseman and said to be brave, a native of Valladolid or of Tudeal de Duero, and he was married to a lady called María de Valenzuela. He was a captain in the island of Cuba, and a rich man, though reputed to be very mean.'

The arrival of Narváez with a numerically superior force threatened the successes which Cortés had so brilliantly won. But Cortés, though faced with this danger of a war on two fronts and fearing that sooner or later the Aztec armies would overwhelm his force by sheer weight of numbers, still had certain advantages which he skilfully exploited. First, there was the technical superiority in arms and armour and in particular the superiority exercised by cavalry over warriors who had never before seen a horse. Secondly, there were the alliances offered by the various Indian tribes whom the Aztecs had recently subdued but not conciliated, and who were quick to grasp this chance of paying off old scores. Thirdly, there was the bewilderment and paralysis of the Aztecs' own will to resist on account of Montezuma's belief that the coming of the white men, and their eventual lordship of the land, had been foretold in the traditional religious lore of his people.[1] Montezuma thus let himself fall tamely into the power of the Spaniards who, when the Aztecs did finally turn and attempt to annihilate them, were able to fight their way out of the trap.

As soon as he reached Mexico, Narváez proclaimed to the bewildered Indians that Cortés was a traitor and sent peremptory messages calling upon him to surrender. Cortés, undismayed, turn to face this new challenge. Leaving only a token garrison in the still unsubdued Aztec capital, he hurried by forced marches, and with all the men he could

[1] Not the least extraordinary aspect of this extraordinary war was that Montezuma actually *expected* the arrival at this time of the God Quetzalcoatl, with whom he immediately identified Cortés. See *Cortés and Montezuma*, by M. Collis, London, 1954.

muster, towards the coast. He sent conciliatory messages, but Narváez brushed them scornfully aside. The envoys which Narváez dispatched to him, however, were courteously received, loaded with costly presents, and returned to their master without the assurances they had been sent to obtain, but with tales of the wealth, magnificence and generosity of Cortés which contrasted strikingly with the stinginess of their own captain. Gradually, by bribes and promises and by the magnetism of his personality, Cortés succeeded in winning over many of Narváez's men to his own cause. Then, in a lightning blow at his rival's headquarters, he overwhelmed the feeble resistance offered and secured the person of Narváez himself, who lost an eye in the skirmish. The men of his expedition then passed under the command of Cortés and proved a welcome reinforcement in the cruel fighting which lay ahead before the Aztec capital was finally secured and all resistance crushed.

For three years, Narváez remained the prisoner of Cortés, though for some time he was placed on parole and was always treated with the tact and courteous generosity which distinguished his captor. Finally, after witnessing the terrible recapture and destruction of Tenochtitlán and the ultimate triumph of the Spaniards, he was released with a gift of two thousand pesos in gold. He returned to Spain with protestations of gratitude on his lips but lost little time in blackening the reputation of his rival at Court and in soliciting for himself the command of a fresh expedition which would efface the memory of his humiliation and win him the lordship of cities more splendid than any which had fallen to the conqueror of Mexico. After brooding upon the prospects which the half-discovered lands of the New World still offered to adventurous spirits, his choice fell upon the neglected heritage of Ponce de León. Narváez applied for, and was granted, the Governorship of Florida.

Why, indeed, Florida? What riches could be hoped for where more than one expedition had already foundered? The scholar, Peter Martyr, in commenting on the Spaniards' vain quest for the Fountain of Youth, had remarked that amongst those who firmly believed in its existence was a certain well-to-do lawyer from Española called Lucas Vasquez de Ayllón. In 1520, this same Ayllón had financed a vessel to explore the coast of the continent to the north of the Florida peninsula. His ship made a landfall on the present coast of North Carolina, in a region which the natives called Chicora. Feigning the warmest friendship, the Spaniards lured a party of some one hundred and thirty on board, then treacherously clapped hatches on them and sailed back to Española with the intention of selling them as slaves. Few of the wretched savages survived. One, however, proved to be a man of superior abilities. He was baptised by his masters under the name of Francisco Chicorano, and learned enough of their language to spin fantastic tales, if not of the Fountain of Youth, at least of other marvels to be found in his native land.

He was taken back to Spain with Ayllón, who solicited from the King the rights of conquest and colonization in the wonderland of Chicora where, so Francisco maintained, the King and Queen were giants and ruled over a race of men with fish-scales and tails so long that holes had to be cut in the chairs they sat on. Above all, the savage never tired of declaring, it was a land sparkling with gold and precious stones in unheard-of profusion. Men listened and marvelled at the tales – Narváez perhaps amongst them, for he was then back in Spain – and flocked to join the five ships which Ayllón equipped for his return to the promised land. But when the Spaniards at length set foot again on the Carolina coast, Francisco disappeared into the forest and was never seen again.[1] Narváez, eagerly pressing his suit at court, could little have guessed that by the time the royal

[1] Oviedo: *Historia General*, III, p. 626.

assent was given, Ayllón would be dead and his colony close to extinction.

But if the Spanish adventurers were dazzled and deluded by such fantasies, the Crown viewed matters more circumspectly. The royal commission granted to Pánfilo de Narváez is an interesting and characteristic document.[1] First, it is made abundantly clear that the whole enterprise is to be financed by the petitioner, who is enjoined to establish at least two colonies of a hundred men each and to build three forts (but only of a 'defensive' character). In return, he is granted the right to explore, conquer and settle the vast region vaguely indicated as stretching from Florida to the Río de las Palmas (the Río Grande), with the title of Governor and Captain-General for life and a princely salary and other valuable privileges – all to be enjoyed, of course, only when the conquest had been effected and the new colony established. The principles on which this conquest and colonization were to be achieved are firmly laid down. The royal conscience, the document declares, had been troubled by the brutality and excesses which had hitherto accompanied the business of discovery and conquest. But the Indians must be regarded as subjects of the King no less than their white masters, and they must be treated not as slaves but as free men. They must not be forced to work in the mines or the pearl fisheries or driven from their homes. The Spaniards must carefully explain to them that they came as friends, that their souls might be saved, and the priests attached to the expedition must see that they are not maltreated or exploited. War might be waged on them only as a last resort, with the agreement of the priests and after all means of peaceful persuasion had been tried and failed. Such were the royal commands.

Besides the Governor and Captain-General, the Crown also appointed the other officers of the expedition; the

[1] *Colección de Documentos Inéditos . . . de Indias*, Series I, Vol. X, 40, and Vol. XVI, 67.

Factor or Quartermaster, the Comptroller (Contador), and the Treasurer, charged with seeing that the royal fifth on all captured treasure, together with other dues, taxes, and perquisites, were properly collected for the King. This latter post was conferred upon a seasoned officer of the Italian and French wars, and a grandson of a celebrated conqueror of the Canary Islands, Alvar Nuñez Cabeza de Vaca,[1] who also held the office of Alguacil Mayor, with responsibility for the military discipline of the expeditionary force. This man was destined to play a leading part in the events which followed.

Five Franciscan friars were also attached to the expedition for the conversion of the natives and the spiritual care of the troops, the senior of them enjoying the title of Comisario. Other adventurers of diverse origins had also volunteered for service, amongst them Don Teodoro, a Greek, whose inventiveness was to stand his comrades in good stead in a critical hour, and a prince of Tezcuco, who had aided Cortés against the Aztecs. The Spaniards called him Don Pedro, for what Castillian tongue could get round the unpronounceable name of Tetlahuehuetzquititzin? A few Spaniards brought with them their personal slaves. Amongst these was a certain Moor or negro from Azamor in Morocco, by name Estebanico, who was to experience the most spectacular adventures. A small group of women also accompanied the expedition, resolved to share the hardships and the glories of their husbands.

The total strength of the expedition which set out from Sanlúcar de Barrameda in June 1527 under the command of Pánfilo de Narváez was about six hundred. Though the crossing of the Atlantic was uneventful, one suspects that

[1] Cabeza de Vaca means, literally, 'head of a cow'. The King of Spain bestowed it upon a maternal ancester after the battle of Las Navas de Tolosa in 1212. This man was a shepherd and he had marked with a cow's skull a trail which enabled the Spaniards to outflank and defeat the Moorish army. Alvar Nuñez must have been particularly proud of this legendary feat as he chose to be known himself as Cabeza de Vaca rather than take the name of de Vera, the conqueror of the Grand Canary.

Narváez was already proving a difficult commander for, on arrival at Santo Domingo, then the chief city of the Spanish colonies, nearly one quarter of the men deserted. Narváez sent to Cuba and Trinidad for fresh supplies and recruits, but sixty more men and two ships were lost in a hurricane and the expedition was obliged to winter in Cuba for rest and repairs. At the end of February, they set sail again, four ships and a brigantine, carrying four hundred men and eighty horses, and set course round the western cape of Cuba. A new pilot had been found – Diego Miruelo, whose uncle had guided the ships of Ayllón's expedition along the east coast of Florida. The younger Miruelo also claimed to be well acquainted with those treacherous seas, but he ran his fleet aground before reaching Cuba and the ships lay stranded there for two weeks until a fresh breeze sprang up and the high seas lifted them off the shoals. The ships then steered towards Havana, but a strong off-shore wind prevented them from entering the harbour and drove them northwards, with no time to refit and replenish their supplies, until they found themselves, by accident rather than sound navigation, off the low, island-fringed shore of Florida. The ships coasted along, hoping to strike the mouth of the great land-locked Tampa Bay. At length, on Maundy Thursday, they came to a smaller cove at the far end of which they sighted a cluster of Indian huts. This seemed to Narváez an auspicious day and place to begin his enterprise and he decided to land.

The Spaniards now stood at the threshold of the country which they had come to explore and to conquer. Of its nature and extent they had only the haziest idea. Was it mainland or island? The royal commission to Narváez refers to the Isle of Florida, though more than one pilot had already sailed along its western coast and followed the vast curving littoral all the way to Pánuco[1] and the borders of

[1] Tampico.

Mexico. The Inca Garcilaso,[1] who sixty years later was chronicling the misadventures of another expedition, could even then only say of Florida that 'we are still ignorant as to whether or not it is limited on the north by more lands or by the sea itself. To the east, it is cut off at a place called the Land of the Codfish,[2] but a certain French cartographer states that between Florida and this land lies another which he even calls New France. On the west, it is bound by the provinces of the Seven Cities . . . likewise by the land of the Chichimecas, a most valiant people who dwell along the borders of Mexico.'[3]

Here the shape of the New World is emerging uncertainly though much still lies shrouded in conjecture and fable. One thing, however, had long been certain. Space and distance had not yet settled into perspective (the pilot Miruelo held that they had only to continue down the coast for a few leagues to reach the mouth of the Río Grande) but the new lands the Spaniards were now exploring bordered, sooner or later, on Montezuma's former realm. In size of population and splendour of treasure these lands must surely equal Mexico even if they did not surpass it. Mexico lay potently upon their minds. The marvels which Narváez had beheld, but of whose possession he had been defrauded, still obsessed his imagination and dazzled him with the vision of still greater marvels to come. The myth of Bimini and its youth-giving waters no longer beckoned: the mirage of the Seven Cities had floated away from the Atlantic isles and had not yet reappeared from the unexplored spaces of the distant interior: but the Spaniards never doubted that somewhere near at hand another Tenochtitlán lay ripe for the taking, and kings mightier than Montezuma would soon be forced to bow before them. Still less did Narváez doubt that he could seize these

[1] See below p. 85, and bibliography.
[2] Newfoundland.
[3] *The Florida of the Inca*, trans. by J. G. and J. J. Varnier, Bk. 1, Ch. 2.

41

prizes with a grasp as sure as that of Cortés. He too would play off one Indian prince against another and lead an army of native auxiliaries into battle. He too would give the word and a multitude of Indian braves would scatter before his arquebuses and the sight of charging cavalry, for, as Bernal Diaz put it, 'after God, the horses were ever our salvation'. The same weapons and the same tactics, wielded with a leadership of no less brilliance, could not fail to win the same golden rewards from the Indians of Florida.

So, at least, it seemed to Narváez on that Maundy Thursday of 1528 when he ordered Alonso Enriquez, the Comptroller, to test the temper of the savages by landing on an island in the bay and see how they they would respond to barter. The Indians did not seem particularly hostile, and they traded some fish and joints of venison to the Spaniards. But the following day, when the Governor landed the bulk of his forces on the mainland, he found the Indian settlement deserted. The inhabitants had taken to their canoes during the night and fled. The men set about ransacking their huts, and amongst the fishing nets and other poor possessions came upon a trinket of gold, probably one of the jingling metal plates with which the natives sometimes adorned their breechclouts. At this discovery hopes ran high. The following day, the rest of the expeditionary force was landed, including the surviving horses, forty-two out of the eighty originally shipped, all of them in sorry condition after the hardships of the voyage. In a solemn ceremony, Pánfilo de Narváez unfurled the royal standard and announced that he took possession of the new land in the name of the King. Other grave formalities followed; the proclamation of the Governor's royal commission, the scrutiny of those of the other officers, the pledging of obedience, then the solemn farce of the reading of the prescribed Summons. This explained to the absent Indians the mysteries of the Christian faith and how God had entrusted to the Catholic Imperial Majesty of Don Carlos

42

the privilege of bringing the gospel to the pagans, who would be kindly treated if they submitted quietly but forced into obedience should they resist.

With an arrogant disregard for the spirit of the Summons, and indeed for one of the basic conditions for the success of his expedition, the Governor had neglected to secure a native interpreter, though one might well have been picked up from the slavers who raided the coast of Florida before the coming of Narváez. The next day a group of Indians approached the Spanish camp, and though their words could not be understood, it was clear from their threatening gestures that they bade the intruders begone. But the Spaniards were as yet too strong to be dislodged by force, and the Indians dispersed with signs of anger and defiance. They were men of the Calusa, the warlike tribe which had driven off the colonists of Ponce de León.

The Governor sent out a party of forty infantry and six horsemen to reconnoitre his new domains. They returned with discouraging reports. The country around was an intricate maze of lagoon, marsh, and inland lake, overgrown with a tangle of mangrove trees and, further inland, cluttered with trunks of great trees which lay rotting in the water where they had fallen. The Spaniards' further advance was blocked by an arm of a great bay[1] which seemed to stretch far inland. The reconnaissance party was reinforced and then struck out again with the intention of skirting the shore of this bay. After a march of four leagues, they managed to seize four Indians. The Spaniards could not converse with them, but they showed them some grains of maize and made them understand that they wished to discover where such crops grew. The Indians replied by signs that they would guide them to a village such as they desired. At the end of the bay they reached a settlement which stood amongst maize fields, but the crop was not yet ripe. Here the Spaniards were startled by a gruesome

[1] Probably Tampa Bay.

find; a number of wooden cases which had once contained stores or merchandise from Spain but which the Indians were using as coffins. In each case lay a man's corpse wrapped in painted deerskins. To the Christians, these mummies, preserved in their strange shrouds and wooden cases, smacked of idolatry and they burnt them. But there were other clues in the village which the Spaniards seized upon more hopefully: a few scraps of canvas, plumes like those worn in Mexico, and some traces of gold. Where had these things come from, the Spaniards asked? From a province not far away, the Indians gave them to understand, which was rich in everything, a land of unbelievable plenty. Its name was Apalache. Could this be the new promised land which the Spaniards were convinced would sooner or later be theirs? Taking with them a few of the Indians, they pushed on to the next village where the reports seemed to be borne out by the sight of more maize fields, now ripe for harvesting. The Spaniards decided to turn back and report to the Governor what they had heard and seen.

Narváez summoned a council of war to decide what should be done. He proposed, he said, to strike inland with his whole force, and to send the ships along the coast until they struck the harbour which the pilots confidently predicted to be very near. The other officers gave their votes in favour of this plan, except for the cautious notary, Hierónimo Alaniz, and Cabeza de Vaca, the Treasurer. The latter, in particular, vigorously dissented, insisting that they must first find a safe harbour for the ships and that it would be wiser to re-embark and sail on up the coast until they found a good anchorage and a country more suited to colonization or effective military operations. The pilots, he declared, did not know where they were and even disagreed amongst themselves; the horses were too weak to be of any military value; there was no means of communicating with the natives or learning something about the nature of the country. Above all, there were no supplies to support an expedition through hostile and desolate country. Heated words were exchanged. To re-embark in the battered ships, after the perils of the long voyage, the Comisario declared, bolstering his lack of military experience with a theological argument, 'would be to tempt God'. It would merely be common prudence, retorted the Treasurer, who called upon the notary to make formal record that he had protested against the rash plans of the Governor.

Narváez defended himself with insults. If the Treasurer was so daunted by the prospect of a hard march, he asserted, let him stay behind in command of the ships and the women, and take them where he could found a settlement in safety. Cabeza de Vaca was greatly affronted. When tempers had cooled and the Governor repeated in friendlier words that he should take command of the ships, as none could be trusted to carry out this difficult task so well, Cabeza de Vaca still persisted in his refusal. To leave the ships and march inland, he repeated, would be to court disaster. 'For I held it to be sure and certain,' he maintained, 'that he [Narváez] would never see the ships again, nor would the ships see him, and this I believed as the expedition was so ill-equipped. But I wished to face even greater dangers than he or the others would face, and endure whatsoever they endured, rather than take charge of the ships and cause people to say of me that because I opposed the expedition I stayed behind out of fear, and thus my courage be called in question; and that I would rather risk my life than see a slur on my honour.'[1] So the ships set sail, but without the Treasurer, who went with the main body of the expedition. The Spaniards struck inland with a desperate defiance

[1] 'Naufragios' of Cabeza de Vaca, Ch. 4. Apart from a report drawn up by the three Spanish survivors and published in Oviedo's Historia, Cabeza de Vaca is the sole authority for the events of the Narváez expedition. His Naufragios are published in Colección de Libros y Documentos referentes a la Historia de America, Madrid, 1906: English trans. is Spanish Explorers in the Southern United States, 1528-1543, ed. by F. W. Hodge, 1907.

stilling the voice of foreboding, and with golden visions of the treasure and food in abundance which awaited them in Apalache.

All but one of the ships, which was wrecked on the treacherous coast, did eventually reach safety. But they never managed, as Cabeza de Vaca had predicted, to discover a trace of the land party, though they searched for a year amongst the arms of Tampa Bay and the maze of islands, creeks, and coastal swamps to the south. For the most part they avoided all contact with the natives, rightly fearing their open hostility or feigned friendship. We know of one group of four who accepted the Indians' offer to come ashore and were then made to run the gauntlet, while the Indians shot arrows at them. The chief of this tribe had every reason to hate the Spaniards: Narváez, or one of his captains, had seized him, had his nose cut off, and then forced him to witness his own mother being torn to pieces by savage dogs. Three of the Spaniards succumbed while the fourth, a lad named Juan Ortiz, was reprieved on account of his youth after being grilled over a slow fire. He later escaped to the territory of a neighbouring chief where he was given asylum, and turned native. He was found eleven years later by de Soto,[1] and provided his expedition with what Narváez had so unhappily lacked – a reliable interpreter and go-between with the natives.

When the ships had set sail, the main body of the army set off inland. They numbered three hundred, including forty mounted men, officers and priests. Each man carried with him two pounds of biscuit and half a pound of bacon, which, eked out with the small and bitter palm nuts they gathered on the way, were their main sustenance during the two weeks' march to Apalache. It was desolate, sandy country, flecked with innumerable lakes and swamps, and intersected with alligator-infested rivers which had to be forded or crossed on rafts. On the far bank of one of these

[1] See p. 87 below.

larger rivers, the Spaniards came upon a band of Indians, some two hundred strong. The Governor went forward to parley with them by signs. Four or five Indians were seized and led the Spaniards to a village where the famished soldiers fell thankfully upon a store of maize. Their route led due north, towards the base of the peninsula. But the need to retain some lines of communication with the coast, and a harbour where ships could bring supplies and reinforcements, still haunted the mind of the Treasurer. Narváez at length yielded to his persuasions and grudgingly allowed him to lead a reconnaissance party back to the coast. But though the sea was not far away, the bays and inlets they found were too shallow to offer any safe anchorage. The water was navigable only by the swift Indian canoes which the Spaniards glimpsed from time to time with their crews of naked warriors whose waving feather headdresses betokened they were bent on war. The sea could bring the Spaniards no help. Their hope was now in Apalache, which lay before them with its promised riches.

At length, as the Spaniards marched on, their ears were startled by an eerie music. Coming towards them they saw a band of Indians playing on reed pipes as they escorted their chief who was arrayed in a painted deerskin and carried, for greater dignity, on the back of a native servant. From the gestures he made to them, the Spaniards gathered he was an enemy of the men of Apalache, and that he would help them against that place. On this chief, who told them his name was Dulchanchelin, they bestowed sundry beads and bells and other trifles, while he presented them with his painted deerskin in token of friendship. Could this be at last what they hoped to find, as Cortés had found in Mexico – a friendly and powerful Indian chief who would furnish them with auxiliaries and carriers in their war against a common enemy? Dulchanchelin led them to the banks of a river, deeper and swifter than any they had yet seen.[1]

[1] In all probability the Suwanee.

Fearing to entrust themselves to rafts, they built rough canoes and spent a whole day in ferrying the army across. One horseman grew impatient at the delay and rode his horse into the stream. But the current was so strong that he was swept out of his saddle and both horse and rider were drowned. The Spaniards grieved over his death, for it was the first loss they had suffered. But the body of the horse was recovered and provided supper that night.

The next day they reached Dulchanchelin's village. Maize had been put out for them, but the place was deserted and they left again without so much as setting eyes on any of the inhabitants. An arrow was loosed after them from a thicket. When they had gone further, they caught sight of Indians hovering in their rear with hostile intent. The Spaniards laid an ambush for them and managed to seize two or three whom they forced to act, sullenly enough, as guides as they pushed on through thickening forests.

The Spaniards were now approaching the base of the Florida peninsula and were veering eastwards towards the Indian settlement of Apalache, somewhere in the neighbourhood of the present town of Tallahassee. Some leagues to the south, the coast curved round to form what is still known today as Apalachee Bay. The Indians of this region were of a different tribe, more civilized, though no less formidable in war, than the primitive Calusa, and richer in the worldly goods most prized by the Indians – maize, coarse bowls in which to pound the grains, deerskins, and small roughly woven cloths. But Apalache itself proved to be no more than a settlement of forty low, straw-thatched huts, built in a clearing surrounded by lofty trees. There were only women and children there when the Spaniards entered, but soon the men came running up shooting their arrows in fury against the intruders and killing one of the horses, before they could be beaten off. A few hours later they were back, making professions of peace and demanding the return of their wives and children. To this the Spaniards

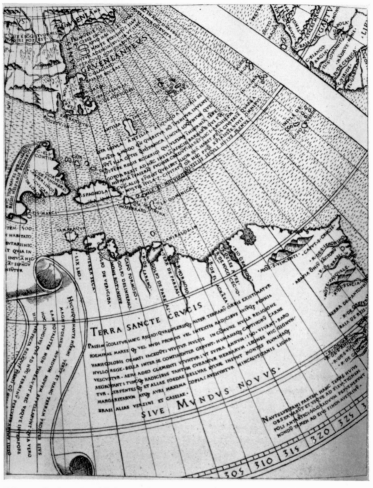

Map of the world by Johann Ruysch (circa 1508) marking the mythical Antillia, or Island of the Seven Cities, in the Atlantic midway between Española (Haiti) and the Azores.

Scenes representing incidents in the Spanish expeditions to Central America and Florida (with portrait of Ponce de León in the right-hand bottom inset).

agreed, but kept a captured chief as a hostage. The following morning, the men of Apalache were before the village again, clamouring for the release of their chief, discharging storms of arrows, and even managing to set fire to the huts. When the Spaniards sallied out against them, the Indians disappeared in the cover of the woods and maize fields. A similar attack followed the day after, but the Indians again vanished into the maize before the Spaniards could do them much injury.

Could this mean settlement be the city rich in gold that the Spaniards had looked to find? Instead of the teeming, docile population of an Indian capital, there were only these bands of ferocious and elusive warriors with their feather headdresses and deadly bows. For three weeks the Spaniards stayed on in the captured village, hoping that the foraging and reconnaissance parties would return with tidings of something better. Narváez earnestly questioned the captive chief and the few friendly Indians who had accompanied him against the Apalachians. They replied with one voice that of all places in the land Apalache was the largest and the richest, and that beyond it there stretched a wilderness of lake and forest where only a few poor tribesmen roamed. But towards the sea, nine days' march away to the south-west, lay another village almost as rich called Aute. Here they would find sea-fish and maize, beans and gourds; a treasure not to be despised by men who had now devoured most of the hoarded grain of Apalache.

The Spaniards' position in the captured settlement was becoming daily more untenable. If the Indians lacked the weight of arms and numbers to eject them by force, they could at least harrass them by a merciless guerrilla warfare. They would lie in wait in a thicket or in a clump of rushes and send their arrows to strike down the Spaniards who ventured out in search of water or forage. Narváez lost many of his men in this way, amongst them Don Pedro, the Mexican Prince who had led his men across the great lake of Tenochtitlán with the army of Cortés, only to perish ignominiously in this distant wilderness of Florida.

When the Spaniards decided to evacuate Apalache the Indians gathered their forces to annihilate them. The lakes and swamps, most terrible of obstacles to the heavily-armed Spaniards, seemed nature's special gift to the natives who, after discharging their arrows, would plunge into the shallow waters and re-emerge to attack from another quarter. The Spaniards' rusting armour was less of a help than a hindrance in such a terrain and against such tactics. The Indians could shoot with deadly effect from a range of up to two hundred paces, and they left off fighting only when their supply of arrows gave out.

After nine days the Spaniards reached Aute. They found it deserted and all the huts burnt down, but in the fields were quantities of gourds and beans, all ripe and ready for picking. Beyond Aute lay the sea, but between stretched the same endless no-man's land of salt marsh and lagoon and low mangrove-tangled island. Parties were sent out to find a way through to the open sea, but the search proved fruitless and the only consolation was the discovery of an abundant oyster-bed, 'at which', says Cabeza de Vaca, 'our people rejoiced greatly, and we rendered heartfelt thanks to God for having brought us thither'. To such straits had the seekers after gold come that the chance find of a few oysters now seemed to them the greatest of God's blessings!

When they rejoined the main camp, the search party found that a third of their comrades had been struck down by an unspecified sickness, probably malaria. Those who were fit enough, and who had horses, began to leave the camp secretly. Only by a stern appeal to their honour could the Governor keep his men together. Gradually a desperate resolve gained ground amongst them. To escape from this labyrinth which was neither water nor land, the open sea must somehow be reached; if their ships had gone, then they must build boats. A mad scheme it seemed, 'as we knew not how to build them, nor had we either the tools, irons, forges, tow, tar, or rigging; nor, in short, a single one of the many things required, nor anyone capable of directing the work, and above all, no food to eat whilst they were being built'.

Yet what seemed beyond all possibility was somehow accomplished. One man of their company proved to be a carpenter by trade. Another volunteered to improvise bellows for the furnaces from deerskins and wooden pipes. Spurs, stirrups and crossbows were melted down to provide nails and the crude axes and saws needed for the work of construction. Palm-bark and fibre served as tow, fibre strengthened with hair from the manes and tailes of horses as cords and tackle, pine-gum was distilled for tar by the resourceful Greek Don Teodoro, shirts turned into sails, split saplings into oars, the skins flayed off in one piece from the legs of horses and cured to do duty as water flasks. Food was procured through four successive raids on Aute and eked out with shell-fish gathered perilously within range of the Indian bows, and with the flesh of a horse slaughtered every third day. After nearly seven weeks' toil five boats had been completed. Each could hold almost fifty men, so that between them all the survivors of the expedition, with such clothes and supplies as still remained, could be taken on board. But with such loads the boats were only a few inches clear of the water and too crowded to be properly handled. But necessity compelled the Governor and his men to commit their lives and fortunes to them.

To reach the open sea, several days had first to be spent crossing the shallow arms of the bay which the Spaniards christened, in memory of the mounts they had sacrificed, Bahía de los Caballos or the Bay of the Horses. Near the mouth of this bay, they came to an island where an abandoned Indian village yielded a feast of fish and dried mullet-roe. The Indians, who had fled at the approach of the Spaniards, also left behind them five canoes which the

Spaniards dismantled, using the wood to give their own boats some much needed free-board. Once the open sea was gained, the Spaniards coasted along in a westerly direction, suffering sorely from thirst, as the horse-hide flasks had soon rotted away. Thus they continued for thirty days until, in the extremity of want, they rounded a headland and entered what was probably Pensacola Bay. In this haven they encountered an Indian settlement, where the natives brought out from their huts pitchers of fresh water and a quantity of roasted fish. The Spaniards, in return offered presents of maize and some barter trifles. But at midnight, when the Governor and his officers were seated with the Chief in his hut, the Indians fell upon them, attacking at the same time the sick who were resting as best they could on the shore. Narváez was wounded in the face with a stone. The Chief managed to break out to join his men, leaving in the hands of the Spaniards 'a sable cloak, than which there can be no finer anywhere in the world, for it exhaled a perfume which seemed to be compounded of amber and musk, and so strong that it could be smelt from afar'. The wounded Governor was helped into a boat, while fifty soldiers held the enemy at bay on the beach until the natives had used all their arrows. The next day, the Spaniards revenged themselves by breaking up all the Indian canoes they could find. Their timbers served to feed the fires round which the Spaniards warmed themselves while waiting for a storm to blow itself out.

And so the harrowing voyage continued. Other Indian canoes were sighted and hailed, the occupants responding at first in seeming friendship, but later hurling stones and giving vent to their hostility. Crazed, perhaps, by the torments of thirst, a negro slave and Don Teodoro, the Greek who had made pitch from the pine trees in the Bay of the Horses, insisted on leaving their companions and entering an Indian canoe. Many years later, another band of Spaniards was told that the Greek had settled down amongst the Indians and were shown the dagger which he had once worn. After Don Teodoro's defection, the five boats toiled on until, at length, a cape was sighted, and beyond it the mouth of 'a very great river', whose current turned the salt water into fresh, so that the Spaniards could slake their thirst in the sea. They had come to the Mississippi. It proved a mighty obstacle. Against the onrush of water, coupled with a fresh off-shore breeze, the Spaniards could make but little headway and were in danger of being driven out to sea. For two days and nights they struggled to cross the delta. The boats were scattered, the men worn out.

The expedition, it was clear, now faced disintegration, and the Governor had neither the will nor the power to prevent it. Thin plumes of smoke rising from the coast indicated that they would find Indian settlements to the north of the delta, if only they could make a landfall. Cabeza de Vaca's boat, by tremendous exertions, at last drew within hailing distance of the Governor's, which stood closest inshore. De Vaca shouted that another of the boats was still within sight but in danger of being driven out to sea, and he urged the Governor to make a final effort to recover it. Narváez replied that it was too far off to be rescued and must be left to its fate. Someone else in the Governor's boat called out that if they could not make land by that evening, they would soon die of hunger and exhaustion. The two boats, the Governor's and the Treasurer's, struggled on a short while together in company. But Cabeza de Vaca saw that his boat was falling behind and called to Narváez, who had the strongest oarsmen with him, to take his boat in tow. Narváez refused. Wind and current were now driving the two boats apart, and the Treasurer shouted out to ask what the Governor's last orders were; 'to which he made answer that it was no time for one man to give orders to another, but that it was now for each to do as he deemed best to save his own life, and that was what he proposed to do. And having said this, he drew away in his boat.'

The Treasurer then decided to join up with the other boat which was further out to sea. He let the current carry him towards it, and for four days and nights the two craft sailed on in company, subsisting on a fistful of maize. They soon lost sight of the Governor, and we only know what happened to him from second-hand accounts left by witnesses who did not long survive him. He made landfall at last on the northern side of the delta, where he chanced upon the crew of another of the boats which had run aground. For several days and nights they journeyed on laboriously together, Narváez keeping to his boat and ferrying the shore-party across the larger bays and creeks. One night, when their last reserves of maize and water had been consumed, the boat was blown out to sea and never regained land. With it went Don Pánfilo de Narváez, luckless rival of Cortés and would-be Governor of unsubdued Florida, with his booming voice and red beard, his boasts and blusterings, and his golden visions unfulfilled.

CHAPTER IV

The Odyssey of Cabeza de Vaca

The Treasurer, Alvar Nuñez Cabeza de Vaca, and his companions, one by one, were succumbing to the tortures of their voyage. Narváez had left them behind. They had lost contact with the second boat in a storm, and, before long, all except the master of the boat and the Treasurer himself were lying dead or unconscious in their leaking craft. One night, through the darkness, Cabeza de Vaca thought he heard the sound of breakers ahead. Rousing the master, he seized an oar and tried to head out to sea until daybreak. But a huge wave struck the boat and hurled it to the shore with a thud which shook his shipmates awake and sent them staggering and dragging themselves through the surf to safety.

The Spaniards, now little more than thirty in number, had made this violent landfall by some gullies where they collected rainwater and managed to kindle a fire at which they roasted some maize. When they had eaten, Lope de Oviedo, the strongest of the survivors, went off to climb a tree to gain some idea of the land. The report he brought back was cheering. They were on an island, and it seemed to him that the fields had been grazed by cattle. Could they have reached a land colonized by Spaniards? Oviedo was sent back to have a closer look. He found a track which led to a small Indian settlement. The huts were deserted, for their owners had gone off to look for food. Taking a pot, some fish, and a small dog which he found, he started back to his companions. But the Indians had seen him. They followed, at first two or three of them, then more and more until there were over a hundred. They carried bows and arrows, and – as Cabeza de Vaca frankly recalls – 'whether or not they were truly tall, our fear made them seem to us as giants'. The Spaniards, famished and half dead with exhaustion, were utterly at their mercy. But the Indians seemed to be inquisitive rather than hostile. They squatted down on the shore and gazed at the white men in astonishment. Cabeza de Vaca walked towards them, offering a few trinkets. The Indians came forward and each gave the Spaniards an arrow in sign of friendship. The warriors made them understand that on the morrow they would return with food, for they had none with them.

The Indians kept their word. The food offered was fish and the nut-shaped farinaceous briar-roots which the natives laboriously grubbed up from beneath the water. In the evening they came again with more of the same food. This time, wives and children came with them, delighted at the sight of the trinkets the Spaniards gave them. The following day, further supplies were brought. The Spaniards decided that with these provisions, they could resume their voyage up the coast. But first they had to launch the boat which was lying half buried in the sand. In their still weakened condition, this was almost beyond their strength. A high sea was still running, and when at length they managed to get the boat afloat it was swamped and overturned by a big wave. Three of the Spaniards were trapped underneath it and drowned. The rest were thrown back on the beach more dead than alive.

The plight of the castaways was now even more wretched than before. They had lost three of their number, their boat, their meagre supplies and possessions, even the clothes they had stripped off for the launching. They were bruised and stunned with the buffeting of the sea and utterly cast down. Someone found an ember from their old fire and the naked men tried to comfort themselves by kindling it anew. But so pitiful was their state that the Indians, coming to visit them with food in the evening, turned back in fear at what they saw. The Spaniards tried to explain what had befallen them, pointing to the bodies of their companions which had been washed up on the shore. 'When the Indians saw the disaster which had overtaken us and the straits we now found ourselves in, with such wretchedness and misfortune, they sat down amongst us,' wrote Cabeza de Vaca, 'and were moved by compassion and grief at our sorry fate and set up so loud and heartfelt a lamentation that it could be heard a long way off. This they kept up for more than half an hour. And to see these men, so rude and brutish, grieving so solely over us made me and my companions the more woefully conscious of our plight.' So Cabeza de Vaca describes the scene. Savages weeping over the misfortunes of the strangers who had come to conquer and enslave them – a scene, indeed, not easily paralleled in the epic of the Conquista.[1]

But how long would this compassion of the Indians last? With their last hope of escape gone, could the Spaniards safely trust themselves to the savages? They remembered what their countrymen had suffered when they fell into the hands of the Aztecs, and anxiously debated the question. But necessity left no choice; abandoned to themselves, the Spaniards could not hope to survive more than a few hours. Cabeza de Vaca calmed the misgivings of his comrades as best he could, and made signs to the Indians to take them back to their houses. This seemed to please the natives who set about collecting brush-wood and kindled large fires at intervals along the path which led to their village. 'At each of these fires,' says Cabeza de Vaca, 'we warmed ourselves,

[1] The lamentations of these Indians may not have been due solely to the spontaneous sympathy which Cabeza de Vaca ascribes to them. Later explorers suggest that such was a common custom which earned for the tribe the sobriquet of Weepers. La Salle's men, who came to those parts nearly a hundred and sixty years later, noted that the Indians would preface every complaint or protest they wished to make with half an hour's weeping. See M. Bishop, *The Odyssey of Cabeza de Vaca*, p. 66.

and as soon as they saw we had regained some strength and warmth, they bore us away to the next so rapidly that our feet seemed scarcely to touch the ground.'

When they reached the Indian village, the Spaniards found a hut prepared for them where they were lodged and fed. That night they could get no rest, for the whole village was given over to dancing and merrymaking, and the thought that they might soon be taken away to be sacrificed filled them with terror. But the night passed, and the next day, and no one laid hands on them. Fear and despair gradually gave way to glimmerings of hope. The Treasurer noticed that one of the Indians was wearing a trinket which was not one of those which he had presented to them. He asked where it had come from. From other white men, they answered, who were with Indians in a neighbouring settlement. Thus Cabeza de Vaca learnt that two Captains, Andrés Dorantes and Alonso del Castillo, had also escaped with all their shipmates. From their combined parties, the four strongest swimmers were selected and set out, accompanied by the prayers and anxious hopes of their comrades, to make their way up the coast in quest of the nearest Spanish outpost. For the rest of the Spaniards, who numbered about eighty, the only hope of survival was to be quartered out amongst the Indian villages of the island and try to subsist on their meagre supplies. But cold weather set in and storms prevented the natives from pulling up the roots growing in the shallows. The flimsy native huts offered little protection against the rain and the piercing gales of winter. Slowly the castaways began to die.

Suffering sometimes drove the Spaniards to acts of gruesome desperation. Cabeza de Vaca gives the names of five Spaniards lodged in one hut who 'suffered such extremity that they devoured one another, until there remained only one, who survived as there was no one left to devour him'. The natives, though inured to hunger, began to succumb to a mysterious disease – possibly a form of the cholera which was to decimate the population of Mexico a few years later – which they attributed to the malevolence of the strangers. Voices were raised that the white men should be killed, and the Indians were only turned from this resolve by the wisdom of one of their elders who argued that the strangers could have no miraculous powers of life or death since they would surely use them to keep themselves alive. As it was, disease and starvation had now reduced their numbers from eighty to fifteen. The Spaniards aptly named this place of shipwreck and disaster Misfortune Island. Those who survived stayed there until April, when the Indians decided to cross over to the mainland and go up the coast in search of the oysters and dewberries which were to be their main food for the coming months. With the spring, the Indians began to recover in health and spirits, and forget their past miseries in dancing and merry-making.

No news had come from the four Spaniards selected to search for the nearest Spanish outpost. Fearing (as indeed proved the case) that they had been killed, the remaining Spaniards decided that the time had come to make a bid to escape themselves. Dorantes and Castillo took command of the little band of thirteen desperate men. Cabeza de Vaca was not amongst them, for it was his turn now to lie prostrate with sickness. For more than a year after the others had gone, he had to share the wretched existence of the natives from Misfortune Island. At last he too was able to slip away and join other mainland Indians, amongst whom his fortunes slowly began to mend. He became a sort of pedlar trading his wares – sea-shells shaped like knives, and pebbles which could be used as beads – in return for hides, ochre, and arrow-head flints from the interior, amongst the Indians who were too indolent or bent on their tribal wars to care for such occupations. He became a familiar figure amongst the natives, who would welcome him with food and give him liberty to wander freely as far as forty or fifty leagues up and down the coast. It was a hard life, for like the Indians he went stark naked, in constant peril from storms and cold and hunger, but it offered one overwhelming advantage; it gave him a thorough knowledge of the country and its inhabitants for many miles around, which he would turn to good account when he judged the time ripe to set out on the great trek back to Christian lands.

For four years Cabeza de Vaca plied his wandering trade amongst the Indians. He would have made a bid to escape sooner had he not learned of the existence of another Spanish survivor whom he resolved to wait for and take with him. This was Lope de Oviedo, the man who had once climbed the tree to discover where fate had brought the castaways, and who was still living as a slave of the Indians of Misfortune Island. But Oviedo was a man stouter in frame than in spirit. He could not swim, and feared the rigours of the trek. Time after time he found excuses for not answering the Treasurer's call, and when at length he was prevailed upon to set out, he turned back to his old masters at the first taste of serious hardship. Cabeza de Vaca went on alone. Soon he had news to console him for the loss of Oviedo. Castillo and Dorantes, whom he had long given up for lost, were still alive, though their companions, except for a negro slave called Estebanico, had perished. We can imagine the deep emotion of their meeting in the wilderness. 'We gave heartfelt thanks to God to find ourselves together again,' says Cabeza de Vaca simply, 'and that day was one of the most joyful in our lives.' Once more, the talk was all of how they could escape together. The Indians were in no mind to let them go, for Cabeza de Vaca, no less than the others, was once again obliged to serve them as a slave. They decided to wait for a further six months, when the natives would set out for another part of the country to feast on prickly pears – the dark, egg-sized cactus plant which would be their food for a carefree three months. Other tribes too would gather for the feast, and the

Spaniards could escape to them and go off with their new masters. The prickly pear season came round, but before the Spaniards could carry out their plan, a bitter quarrel broke out amongst the Indians who dispersed in dudgeon, taking their slaves with them. Another year passed before the Spaniards could meet again at the gathering of the prickly pears; a year, Cabeza de Vaca says, of great wretchedness, 'on account both of being famished with hunger and being roughly treated to such an extent that I was forced to escape three times from my masters, whilst they tried to hunt me down to kill me'. But somehow the months went by, the season of plenty came round again, and the Spaniards were able to meet and make their escape together.

The fugitives travelled in peril of their lives. Had they been dependent only on the whims and uncertain hospitality of the various and sometimes ferocious tribes through which they now began to journey, they could scarcely have survived for long. But they discovered themselves to be endowed with unexpected powers. When still in wretched servitude on Misfortune Island, Cabeza de Vaca had been forced by his masters to try his hand at healing the sick. 'Our way of healing,' he relates, 'was to make the sign of the cross over them and to say a *Pater Noster* and an *Ave Maria*, and to pray Our Lord as best we could to restore them to health and to put it into their hearts to treat us well.' The double prayer had proved efficacious; the sick Indians had one and all declared that as soon as the sign of the cross had been made over them they felt perfectly well again, and in gratitude they presented the Christians with whatever food or trifles they possessed. News of the healings which Cabeza de Vaca and other Spaniards had from time to time accomplished had even reached the distant Avavares tribe through whose territories they now wished to pass. The natives came out to meet the mysterious strangers, beseeching them to cure the sick, and offering them shelter and

61

food in abundance. Castillo was at first the one most sought after, and the accounts which Cabeza de Vaca has left us of the cures effected by his unwilling countryman are not without their touches of humour. Fevers, pains in the head, crippled cases even, were plain sailing, though the cures aroused great wonder and excitement. But graver cases were sometimes brought, to the embarrassment of the healer; 'for Castillo was a most timorous doctor, specially in cases where the cure was very dangerous and awe-inspiring; and he feared that his sins would prevent his cures from taking effect.' Cabeza de Vaca was more robust in faith and character; he healed a native who was lying prostrate and given up for dead, and exorcized the vampire-like demon that had long kept a whole tribe in awe. So loud was the clamour of the Indians to benefit from the miraculous powers of the Christians and so great the press of people flocking round, that Dorantes and even the negro Estebanico found themselves obliged to join the healing. The natives declared that the strangers were children of the sun, 'and such was their confidence that they would be healed if we treated them,' Cabeza de Vaca concludes, 'that they believed none of them would die so long as we were there.'

For eight months the Spaniards stayed with these Avavares Indians, and although they were well treated they all suffered from hunger and exhaustion once the season of the prickly pears was over. At the first sign of spring, they slipped away again, first to the Maliacones, then on to the Arbadaos, a poor, sickly tribe who subsisted almost entirely on a fruit which made the mouth burn and excited an intolerable thirst. The Indians were entirely absorbed in the endless quest for food, and the Spaniards did what they could to survive by making combs and by trading bows, arrows and nets. When the Indians bartered them a piece of meat they would eat it raw, for if they squatted down to cook it, the first native who chanced their way would snatch it up and devour it himself. Sometimes they were given raw hides to soften by gnawing them. 'The greatest good fortune I enjoyed at that time,' Cabeza de Vaca writes, 'was when they gave me something to scrape, for I went on scraping and scraping and devoured the shreds I tore off, and that sufficed for three or four days.' Life amongst such poverty-stricken savages was hard and brutal indeed. Like them, the Spaniards went stark naked, and as they were not used to it, they shed their skins twice a year 'like snakes'. They developed too a painful rash on their chests and backs, which the loads of firewood they were obliged to carry made raw and inflamed. This fetching of brushwood through the thick scrub was a constant agony in which, Cabeza de Vaca relates with patient piety, 'I had no other help or consolation but to think on the passion of Our Redeemer Jesus Christ, and in the blood He shed for me, and to reflect how much greater must have been the torment which He suffered from the thorns than what I was then suffering.'

To regain their strength before passing on to the next tribe, the Spaniards allowed themselves a treat. They bartered from the Indians two small dogs, which afforded them a substantial meal. For the following days, their diet was cactus-leaves roasted all night over a camp fire until they were soft enough to eat. In the next settlements they encountered, the Indians were frightened at the strange aspect of the Spaniards, but proved friendly enough once their sick had been brought out for healing. The tribe beyond enjoyed greater fortune, for they lived off a plentiful supply of mezquite-beans, which furnished a great feast, with much dancing and revelry, in honour of the strangers. The way, though still long and arduous, was beginning to take on the character of a triumphal march.

They came to the shores of a river, 'as broad as the river at Seville'; it was the Rio Grande. From the settlement which lay beyond, 'the entire population came out to receive us with a tremendous noise of shouting and much slapping of thighs'. The Indians bore with them their sacred instruments—gourds hollowed out and filled with stones which they would rattle with pious fervour to mark some solemn event. So great was the excitement of the natives and their eagerness to touch the healers, that the Spaniards were forced to seek safety in the huts prepared for their reception and to withdraw from the frenzied revels until the morrow when, after making the sign of the cross over them, they resumed their journey accompanied by the entire village.

And so they continued, meeting everywhere with the same reception; food and hides, beads and arrows – whatever trifles of value the Indians possessed – being piled before them that they might heal the sick and make the miraculous sign of the cross over them. At one village they found the inhabitants suffering from an eye disease, some of them being quite blind. At another, Cabeza de Vaca removed with his knife an arrow-head which an Indian carried embedded in his chest for many years, and sewed up the wound with thongs of leather. This feat increased the veneration with which the Spaniards were regarded. A medicine-man presented them with two of the sacred gourds, which they henceforth carried with them as a symbol of authority. But the gift which most gladdened them was a copper bell, ornamented with a face. This, the Indians said, had come from the north, where many other such things were to be found. Whatever its country of origin might be, the Spaniards knew that the inhabitants must be familiar with the art of smelting and working metal. Could this clue point to another land, rich and populous as the empire of Mexico? The vision which the cruel realities of the wilderness had driven from their mind began once more to glimmer.

Once the four travellers, with their Indian escort, had crossed the Rio Grande, they were within the boundaries of present-day Mexico. But an obstacle mightier than the river now barred their way. The flat lands over which they had marched all the way from their first landing in Florida more than six years before now dramatically gave way to a chain of mountain ranges which barred their way to the south. They could, it is true, have skirted the mountains by taking a route to the east, and this would have led them most directly to Pánuco and Christian lands. But it would also have led them back to the coastal lowlands, and to the fierce and brutish natives akin to those amongst whom they had so long suffered servitude. Better to keep amongst the gentler tribes of the interior, where the Spaniards were now feted and revered as demigods, even though they might for a time be forced to take a circuitous route to the west. There was now, too, another consideration which weighed the more heavily with them as they drew nearer to their goal: 'by taking the overland route, we could note many of its features, for if the Lord should be pleased to deliver us of our foes and bring us to a Christian land, we might give an account of it.' So the decision was made, and the indomitable travellers headed west for a trek of a further two thousand miles before they were to meet with other men of their own race.

It is not easy from this point to follow their course with any certainty. Cabeza de Vaca himself, in his record of it, admits that the task is beyond him, for 'we journeyed on through so many sorts of people, of such diverse languages, that memory cannot recall them.' The course shifted at length from west to north, for again a mountain range barred the way, and forced them to cross the desert lands of Coahuila and come at length, for the second time, to the deep gorge of the Rio Grande. This they recrossed by fording, and headed again for the west. Everywhere the Indians received them with awe and reverence. Sometimes they would pray the holy men to remain with them, or at least they would try to deny the enemies of their tribe the inestimable boon of a like visitation. But the white men insisted always that they must be led towards the setting sun, and when, on one occasion, the Indians still stubbornly demurred, the chief of the white men records that 'we grew angry, and I went one night to sleep in the fields away from them'. The results of the Spaniards' displeasure were unexpected and tragic. 'All the night they stayed awake and kept entreating us not to be angry any more, for though they would die on the road they would lead us where we wished to go. And as we still feigned to be angry, lest their fear should forsake them, there happened a very strange thing which was that the very same day many of them fell ill, and on the next eight of them died. Wherever this was known throughout the land they stood in such awe of us that it seemed they would drop dead at our very sight. They implored us to put away our anger (nor indeed did we want any more of them to die) and they firmly believed we were killing them merely by wishing them to die. But in truth our distress at what was happening could not have been greater, for not only did we behold some of them dying, but we feared they might all die or abandon us out of fear, and that from then onwards all the other Indians we came to would do the same, seeing the fate that had befallen these.' But mercifully the danger passed, and all was well. 'We prayed our Lord for His help; and thus all those who had fallen sick began to get well.'

When the sick had recovered, the long journey was resumed, Castillo and Estebanico the negro going on ahead through desolate country. After some days they returned with heartening news; they had found a settlement where the Indians dwelt in well-built huts and lived on beans and gourds. Some maize, too, had been seen – the first since Florida. The whole population came out to welcome them. The Spaniards found them to be a strong and handsome people of lively intelligence, living mainly off the herds of buffalo which roamed the great plains, to the verge of which they had now come. With these friendly people the Spaniards rested a few days, deliberating which way they

should take; the 'direction of the cows', which led northwards across the plains, or 'towards the sunset' and the lands
where maize grew. They chose the latter course and set out
once more. Forty-seven years later, a Spanish expedition in
search of some lost Franciscan friars, chanced upon the same
village and reported with astonishment that 'these people
seemed to have some light of our holy faith, for they made
signs of God, looking up to heaven, and came to the friar
(which the captain and soldiers brought with them) that he
might bless them.'[1] When questioned as to how they had
received such Christian knowledge, they replied that they
had it from three white men and a negro who dwelt a few
days with them many years ago.

After leaving the friendly settlement where their memory
was to be cherished for so long, the Spaniards journeyed on
until they came again, for the third time, to the Rio Grande.
They followed its eastern bank for many a day, then struck
out again across the desert, journeying from water-hole to
water-hole and subsisting on nothing but the ration of venison fat they carried with them for such an emergency. They
came at last to a region so seared and poor that the inhabitants, and the Spaniards themselves, Cabeza de Vaca says,
were forced to make do with a diet of powdered straw.

[1] *Colección de Documentos inéditos de America*, XV, p. 107; translation
from Hakluyt: *Navigations*, IX, p. 191.

But such extremities of hardship now meant little to them; they were inured to hunger and exhaustion, almost beyond the reach of earthly suffering, and their miraculous fortitude served only to increase the aura of their divine authority amongst the Indians. 'Whilst travelling,' Cabeza de Vaca records, 'we went without food all day until night, and we ate so little as to astonish them. We never felt weariness, neither were we indeed at all weary, so schooled were we to hardship. We possessed great influence and authority; to preserve both, we seldom talked with them. The negro was our go-between; he informed himself about the ways we wished to take, what towns there were, and the matters we desired to know.' At length, after leaving the land of the straw-eaters, it needed none of Estebanico's interpreting to tell them that the worst of their odyssey now lay behind them. Richer lands were once more at hand; behind the hills stretched fields of maize and beans and gourds, and villages where folk dwelt in houses made of earth and reed mats and clothed themselves in cotton wraps.

For more than a hundred leagues the Christians travelled on through this land, heartened by the evidence of increasing prosperity. Food was plentiful, the cotton robes of the Indians seemed to be of even finer quality than those worn in Mexico, and the ornaments which they freely bestowed on the strangers betokened more trade and a higher degree of civilization than they had yet encountered. In one settlement the inhabitants laid before Dorantes an offering of six hundred deer-hearts, on account of which the Spaniards called the place Pueblo de los Corazones. Nor were the hearts of deer the people's only wealth. They had coral beads from the South Sea, turquoises, and arrow-tips of emerald which they used in their ceremonial dances. Where did these things come from, the Spaniards asked? From beyond the mountains to the north, answered the Indians; they had traded them for parrots' feathers from folk who lived in towns – in towns built of great mansions. These words set the Spaniards wondering. From the north, again – from the same land where, they had learned, men knew the art of smelting metal? And what manner of men could those be, who dwelt in towns, in great mansions? But it would have to be for others to unveil such mysteries; the four travellers had had their fill of strange lands and stranger peoples. Their trails now led not to the north, but almost along the shore of the Pacific Ocean to the Spanish settlements in the south.

Suddenly a sign was vouchsafed that their goal was not far distant. While they were waiting for a river in spate to subside, Castillo noticed that one of the Indians was wearing a strange ornament round his neck. He looked closer; it was a buckle from a sword-belt and, sewn inside it, a horse-shoe nail! The Indian declared that the strange objects had come from heaven. On being pressed further, he explained that they had been brought by bearded men who had carried lances, with which they had wounded some Indians. Then they had ridden back into the sunset.

Who were these Spaniards, and where had they come from? Were they the frontier patrols of some settlement, or just a band of raiders who had made their way inland on a slaving expedition? The four travellers anxiously discussed the question as they travelled on. Soon they found an answer in the nature of the country. Fertile it still remained, but so ravaged and abandoned that 'we were moved to great compassion to see the land most fair and fertile, abounding in lakes and rivers, but the villages despoiled and deserted, and the people who had fled and gone into hiding so lean and ill, for as they did not sow, their raging hunger drove them to live off roots and the bark of trees.' The Indians told them that half the men, and all the women and children, had been carried away into slavery. At first, Cabeza de Vaca and his companions feared that the desperate natives might wreak vengeance on them when they learned they were of the same race and faith as the marauders. But to their relief and wonder, the Indians brought out from their hiding places the furs they had concealed from the slavers and offered them as gifts, for they venerated the strangers no less than had the other Indian tribes; 'the which,' Cabeza de Vaca sagely concludes, 'clearly shows that to bring these people to the Christian faith and the service of the Imperial Majesty, they should be won over by good treatment, and that this is the proper way, and no other.'

The Indians led their guests to a village which stood on the spur of a lofty hill, well beyond the reach of invaders. Here hidden stores of maize were brought out which the Spaniards distributed amongst the famished Indians who escorted them. From this mountain refuge messengers were sent out in all directions to summon the people to meet. But the days passed and the messengers returned to report that the country was deserted. Those who had escaped enslavement had gone into hiding. The messengers had seen a band of white men leading away a string of captives in chains. At this news, many of the Indians accompanying Cabeza de Vaca wanted to turn back, and only with difficulty could he allay their fears. Soon, there was unmistakable evidence that the messengers had spoken the truth. In a clearing they found stakes where, only a night or two before, other white men had tethered their mounts. It was a moment of deep emotion. Here was the sign that their seven long years in the wilderness were at an end, and that the wanderers had returned to their people.

Cabeza de Vaca, ever to the fore in eagerness of spirit, went on ahead of his companions with the negro and a few Indians. After three days of forced marches they came up with the mounted raiding party who, de Vaca tells us and we can easily believe him, were 'dumbfounded to see me so strangely clad and in the company of Indians. For a long while they stood gazing at me without speaking a word'.

The raiding party Cabeza de Vaca had fallen in with was led by a ruffian called Diego de Alcaráz. They were in quest of slaves, and when, a few days later, Dorantes and Alonso del Castillo came up with a retinue of some six hundred Indians, they were filled with resentful and covetous amazement. 'Many disputes arose between us,' Cabeza de Vaca records, 'as they would have us reduce the Indians we brought with us to slavery.' The Indians refused to be separated from their revered leaders, and when Alcaráz threatened and cajoled them through his interpreters, claiming that his party were the lords of the land who must be obeyed and served, the Indians not only refused to listen to them, but stoutly maintained that they could not be of the same kin as the four workers of miracles since 'we had come whence the sun rises, and they whence it sets; we healed the sick, whereas they killed the sound; we had come naked and barefoot, while they had come clothed, mounted, and with lances; that we were not covetous of anything but would forthwith give up everything that was bestowed on us, whilst the others were only bent on robbing whomsoever they found.'

Only with the greatest difficulty were the Indians persuaded to part from their holy men, who had still many miles to go before reaching the first Spanish settlement. Alcaráz swore that the natives had nothing to fear, but as soon as Cabeza de Vaca and his companions had taken an affectionate farewell of the bulk of their followers, the slavers threw scruples to the winds and seized all they could lay hands on. 'Whereby it may be seen,' Cabeza de Vaca bitterly reflects, 'how men may be deceived of their hopes. For we had been bent on securing the liberty of the Indians, and when we thought we had achieved it, the very reverse occured, as the Spaniards were resolved to fall on the Indians whom we had sent peacefully and trustingly away, and they did as they had resolved.'

Not all the Spaniards in this unsettled frontier region however were of this stamp, and in Melchior Díaz, the officer in command of the outpost town of Culiacán, in

Sinaloa, to whom the four wanderers were now led, Cabeza de Vaca found a man whose word he could trust. Díaz besought him to use his influence with the local natives to get them to return to their deserted villages and untilled fields, and gave his solemn promise that they would be left undisturbed. The few Indians who had remained to escort Cabeza de Vaca were dispatched through the country, this time bearing one of the sacred gourds which had served as the symbol of the healers' authority, to summon the people back to their homes. After a few days they returned with three chiefs bringing gifts of beads and turquoises and feathers. Slowly their people followed. Cabeza de Vaca exhorted them to return to their homes, and whenever a band of Spaniards approached, to come out to greet them with crosses in their hands and gifts of food. Melchior Díaz in turn bestowed presents on them in token of peace and good faith, and the pact of friendship was sealed in due formality by a Spanish notary. This done, Cabeza de Vaca went on his way, for a hundred leagues of desert still separated him from Compostela, the seat of the Governor Nuño de Guzmán. And as he went, reports were brought to him that the Indians were indeed settling again in their villages and had begun to raise crosses, and even churches, as he had exhorted them.

At last, at the beginning of June 1536, the wanderers reached Compostela and were brought before the Governor. Cabeza de Vaca, for all his years in the wilderness, could hardly have been ignorant of the reputation which Nuño de Guzmán had won for himself in the Indies. A bitter rival of Cortés, he had raised a large army of Aztecs and Tlascaltecs and started seven years before to explore and conquer the north-west, to which the name of Nueva Galicia was later given. He subdued the natives with unspeakable barbarity, founded the outpost of Culiacán, and would have pushed on beyond but for the barrier of mountain and desert which barred his way. Feared and hated, Guzmán had hitherto ruled and exploited his domains in defiance of all attempts by the Crown to call him to account. Only now was his downfall imminent, and the judges appointed to investigate his conduct were to secure his arrest a few months after Cabeza de Vaca had visited him at Compostela. To the wanderers returning from the desert, Guzmán showed himself unwontedly gracious. He made them gifts of rich attire which, for many days, they were quite unable to wear, so intolerable did all clothing seem to men accustomed to go naked or clad in skins. He listened to the story of their odyssey with deep interest tinged with envy. They had come from those lands beyond the mountains and deserts which he himself had striven to find, and which he still believed to be rich in gold and silver, and their tales brought him confirmation of a legend that had once haunted him. This legend is described in a celebrated passage by the chronicler Pedro de Castañeda:[1] 'In the year 1530, Nuño de Guzmán, who was President of New Spain, had in his possession an Indian, a native of the valley or valleys of Oxitipar, who was called Tejo by the Spaniards. This Indian said he was the son of a trader who was dead, but that when he was a little boy his father had gone into the back country with fine feathers to trade for ornaments, and that when he came back he brought a large amount of gold and silver, of which there is a good deal in that country. He went with him once or twice, and saw some very large villages, which he compared to Mexico and its environs. He had seen seven very large towns which had streets of silver-workers. It took forty days to go there from his country, through a wilderness in which nothing grew except some very small plants about a span high. The way they went was up through the country between the two seas, following the northern direction . . . towards the country named "The Seven Cities".'

[1] *Spanish Explorers in the Southern United States*, edited by F. W. Hodge and T. H. Lewis, Barnes and Noble (1907) pp. 285-6.

CHAPTER V

Rivals in the Quest

The Seven Cities! The phrase had a magic about it, stirring memories of the ancient legend of Antillia and its lost Christian communities, a legend now unaccountably transplanted, as the explorers rolled back the frontiers of human knowledge, to the depths of inland America. By what strange alchemy of mind had the tales told by Tejo the Indian become fused with the myth of Antillia and its seven cities we can only guess. Within a decade or two of the voyages of Christopher Columbus, men were beginning to wonder whether the Seven Cities, of which no trace had been found on the islands recently discovered, might perhaps lie somewhere on the mysterious mainland. Although some cartographers continued to indicate the mythical Antillia on their maps until well into the second half of the sixteenth century – Michael Lok's map of 1582 shows a forlorn little island marked *Sept Cites*, and a similar feature appears in the Ortelius map of 1570, and Mercator's of 1587 – the Seven Cities were already transplanted to mainland America some four years before Ponce de León's first attempt to find the Fountain of Youth. A map of the world thought to have been drawn in 1508[1] shows the cities (represented by the conventional indication of mitres) strung vaguely along the eastern sea-board of the American mainland over an area ranging from west of the Tierra de Bacallaos (Newfoundland) to a point nearly opposite the west end of Cuba – far removed indeed from the lands to be explored by Cortés and Guzmán, but nevertheless on the mainland.

[1] Now in the British Museum.

The Indians too had legends of their own, and most probably it was one of these which, through mutual incomprehension and conjecture, became merged in the Spaniards' imagination with dimly-remembered myths of their own. Many tribes of Mexico and Central America cherish tales of how their race issued from Seven Cities – the Chicomoztoc of Nahuatl folklore, the Tulan Zuiva in the Quichi tradition of Guatemala. Fray Juan de Zumárraga, the first Bishop of Mexico and himself a fervent supporter of the quest for the Seven Cities, caused great numbers of Indian myths to be carefully collected, and they were later published in the *Historia de los Mexicanos por sus pinturas*. In this work Chicomoztoc appears as a place where the Mexican tribes rested for a number of years in their migratory wanderings. It is similarly mentioned in the *Anales de Cuanhitlan*, another famous collection of Indian legends collected some thirty years after the conquest. Everything suggests, in short, that the Indians of Mexico preserved a tradition that, at some stage in their history, their ancestors had dwelt in seven distinct but associated communities beyond the borders of their present homeland. In these seven caves, groups, or communities, the Spaniards may have thought they recognized the re-emergence of their own legend of the Seven Cities.[1] So firmly and speedily was this identification achieved, that within a year or two of listening to the tales of the Indian Tejo, the quest for the Seven Cities had become the main goal of Nuño de Guzmán's expeditions.[2]

But now Guzmán's days of exploring, marauding, and

[1] For an interesting discussion of this subject see *Contributions to the History of the south-west portion of the United States*, by A. F. Bandelier, Papers of the Archaeological Institute of America, American Series, V. (Cambridge, U.S.A., 1890, pp. 6 *et seq.*)

[2] 'The goal of our journey when we set out to explore this river was the Seven Cities, since the Governor Nuño de Guzmán had tidings of them, and of a river which flowed out into the South Sea, and which was 4 or 5 leagues in width.' *Segunda Relación Anónima de le Jornada de Nuño de Guzmán, Colección de Documentos para la Historia de Mexico*, Ycazbalceta, Vol. II, p. 303, quoted by Bandelier op. cit., p. 15.

slaving were all but over and he could only listen to Cabeza de Vaca's extraordinary adventures and let him proceed to Mexico City, where he arrived on 23 July, 1536, to report to the Viceroy, Don Antonio de Mendoza. Mendoza, a nobleman of integrity and ability, had been sent out by the Crown to suppress abuses and establish the royal authority. He had been less than a year in his new capital and was not finding his task an easy one. Cautious, yet determined to miss no opportunity of extending his royal master's power and domains, he received de Vaca, Castillo and Dorantes graciously and listened with close attention to everything they had to tell him.

After resting for two months in Mexico City, Cabeza de Vaca decided that he would return to Spain. It seems probable that Mendoza sounded him to see whether he would be prepared to lead an expedition, in the Viceroy's name, back to the lands through which he had passed. But Cabeza de Vaca had other plans. He wished to present himself at Court and solicit the rights of conquest for himself. He was delayed in Mexico throughout the winter by the difficulty of securing a passage but he was able to set sail at last in the spring of 1537. Castillo made no secret of the fact that he had had enough of wandering, married a wealthy widow, and retired peacefully into private life. Dorantes seems to have hesitated before following the same course. While waiting at Vera Cruz to take ship to Spain, he received a letter from the Viceroy urging him to return to the capital. There Mendoza offered him the command of a small expedition, to be composed of friars and soldiers. Dorantes accepted, then withdrew, and the project came to nothing. The Viceroy reported the circumstances some-what peevishly to the Emperor: 'I have spent a great amount of money on the expedition, but for reasons I do not know it has all come to nought. From all the preparation I have made there are left to me only a Negro who came with Dorantes, some slaves whom I have purchased, and some

Indians, natives of the country, whom I have assembled."[1]
These Indians, and particularly the Negro, were destined
still to play an important part in the quest for the Seven
Cities. Clearly something more was required before an
expedition could be launched – a leader of enterprise and
integrity; and at about time that Cabeza de Vaca sailed for
Spain, a man arrived in the city of Mexico whom the Bishop,
and soon afterwards the Viceroy himself, considered ideally
suited for this task. This was a Franciscan friar known as
Marcos de Nizza.

Friar Marcos, a Savoyard by origin, had made his way to the
New World and witnessed some of the most spectacular
events of Pizarro's conquest of Peru. Stirred to horror by
the cruelties of the Spaniards, he had sent to Bishop Zumárraga accounts of what he had seen, and it seems probable
that these same reports may have been used by Las Casas
in his famous denunciation of the Conquista, *La Destrucción
de las Indias*. Zumárraga had urged Friar Marcos to come
to Mexico, where the Bishop warmly commended him to
the Viceroy. He was offered and accepted the command
of the expedition.

The Viceroy's instructions to Friar Marcos have been
preserved and reveal the humane and reasonable spirit in
which the expedition was to be conducted – a spirit in close
harmony with Cabeza de Vaca's own attitude to the new
lands and their inhabitants. First, the friar was required 'to
exhort and encourage the Spaniards residing in San Miguel
(Culiacán) to treat well those Indians who are at peace and
not to demand their services for excessive labour'. The
Indians in turn were to be consoled and assured of the
Viceroy's intention to see that they were fairly treated and
would never again be left to the mercies of the slavers. The
Friar should also report how the new Governor, Francisco

[1] Quoted in *Coronado, Knight of Pueblos and Plains*, by H. E. Bolton,
p. 16.

77

Vasquez de Coronado, who had been appointed to succeed Guzmán, was carrying out the Viceroy's instructions in the same sense. Having thus assured law and justice in the frontier lands, Friar Marcos was to proceed with the negro Esteban[1] and the Indian guides to explore the country to the north, pacifying and exhorting the natives as he went and noting 'the kind of people they are, whether numerous or not and if scattered or living together; the quality and fertility of the land, its climate, the trees and plants, domestic or savage animals, the aspect of the land, whether rugged or level, the streams, if large or small, and the rocks and metals'. Wherever possible, he should send back specimens of what he found on the way, and ample despatches to tell how he was faring. In particular, the Friar was to note the lie of the sea-coast, 'for it might be that the continent would grow narrower, and some arm of the sea would enter the land'. He should keep an eye open for larger settlements where monasteries might suitably be founded, and wherever he went he should take possession of the land in the name of His Majesty, 'giving the natives to understand that there is a God in heaven, and the Emperor upon this earth to rule and command them'.[2]

Before he accepted the viceregal commission, Friar Marcos had considered, but finally decided against, entering the service of the man who alone could challenge the Viceroy in prestige and in his zeal for the conquest of the Seven Cities – Don Hernán Cortés. Cabeza de Vaca too had seen Cortés and related his adventures to him. No details are known of what passed between them, but we can be sure that Cortés had listened with the keenest interest, for he himself had made strenuous efforts to probe the mysterious lands to the north.

[1] Estebanico, the former companion of Cabeza de Vaca, now generally referred to as Esteban, rather than by the more familiar diminutive, in recognition of his enhanced status.
[2] Bandelier, op. cit., pp. 109-112.

Not content with having achieved the most spectacular feat of the Conquista (for he had been robbed of its fruits by a jealous Crown) Cortés had pressed on with his discoveries in the South Sea, and his ships were the first to cross the Pacific and reach the Spice Islands. The prize which he most longed for was the discovery of the mythical Northern Straits, the short-cut through the land mass of America by which it was believed that ships could sail from Spain direct to the Spice Islands. 'And even if it be not discovered,' he had written to the Emperor as far back as 1522, 'very great and rich lands cannot fail to be found.' In 1529, he had returned from Spain with the high-sounding title of Marquis of the Valley of Oaxaca and Captain-General of New Spain and of the Southern Coast. But his wings were clipped by the establishment of the Audiencia as the supreme civil authority, and later of the Viceroyalty, in the lands he had conquered. Though he was still permitted to continue his explorations by sea, and did so with great persistence and vision, his ventures had met with only partial success.

While Nuño de Guzmán, excited by Tejo's tales of the Seven Cities, was sending his marauding expeditions overland, Cortés had followed up the same clues by dispatching two ships under the command of his kinsman Diego Hurtado de Mendoza to explore the coast. They reached as far up the coast as about 27 degrees north, before a mutinous crew forced the captain of one of the ships to turn back. How much further Hurtado Mendoza may have reached is not known, for nothing more was ever heard of him. Cortés sent a second expedition to look for him but this fared scarcely better, for when its commander, Fortuno Ximenes, landed in a small bay, he was set upon by the natives and slain with twenty of his men. The only fruit of the expedition was the report brought back by the survivors that the island abounded in the finest pearls.

Cortés then decided to lead the next expedition in person.

In May 1535 he landed in the bay where Ximenes had been killed and named the place, which he believed to be an island, California. The name had a curious history. Eighteen years after the discovery of America, a romance of chivalry had been published by García Ordoñez de Montalva which became popular with navigators and conquistadores. 'Know then,' the writer had declared, 'that on the right hand of the Indies is an island called California, very close to the Terrestrial Paradise, and it was peopled by Black Women without any man amongst them, for they lived in the fashion of Amazonia. They were of strong and hardy bodies, of ardent courage, and of great strength. Their island was the mightiest in the world, with its steep cliffs and rocky shores. Their arms were all of gold, and so was the harness of the wild beasts which they tamed and rode. For in the whole island there was no metal but gold. They lived in caves wrought out of the rocks with much labour. They had many ships with which they sailed out to other countries to obtain booty.' Though the native women whom Cortés encountered could hardly be described as black, and their arms were certainly innocent of all trace of gold, the island seemed to him to lie 'at the right hand of the Indies'. So California it was called, though the place was a desolate sandy waste, assuredly as far removed as it possibly could be from any terrestrial paradise. There Cortés had remained, amidst the sullen resentment of his soldiers, for more than a year. He had not long returned home when Cabeza de Vaca reached Mexico and talk of the wondrous Seven Cities was once more on every man's lips. Cortés was in all probability already planning to send out another expedition when news reached him that Friar Marcos was in Mexico and might prove a useful recruit. But the Friar refused his offers, and Cortés never forgave him for entering the rival services of the Viceroy.[1]

---

[1] Cortés later claimed that the knowledge which Friar Marcos alleged he gained at first hand about the Seven Cities was in reality only a re-hash

F. Delfinum

Pecu Gallicum

A landing on the coast of Florida.

Indians travelling by canoe.

The following year (1539), after Friar Marcos had set out overland for the Seven Cities, Cortés made his final bid to reach the goal by sea. Three ships were sent under the command of Francisco de Ulloa to undertake a thorough survey of the coast. Ulloa explored both shores of what he called the Sea of Cortés, and made the discovery that the 'island' of California was really a long peninsula. A great river emptied its waters into the head of the gulf. Could this waterway lead to the heart of the land of the Seven Cities? Ulloa could not force his way past the shoals and against the swirling torrent, and he was compelled to sail back without probing its secret. The glory of this discovery was destined neither for him nor for his master, for Cortés himself left the Indies at the beginning of 1540 never to return. The seven years of life which remained to him were spent in disappointment and frustration. Though he accompanied the Emperor in the unsuccessful campaign against Algiers, he was not allowed the chance to show his mettle. What was the reduction of a Moorish stronghold to the man who had overthrown a whole empire? Cortés was never invited into the inmost councils of his native land, his offer to capture Algiers was not taken seriously and the Crown rejected the services of the man who had proved himself to be the ablest soldier-administrator of a great age.

of the information Cortés had passed on to him about conditions along the coast of the Gulf of California. 'And when I returned from the said country (i.e. California) Friar Marcos spoke with me, when I was in New Spain, and I gave him tidings of this said country and its exploration, since I was proposing to send him in my ships to continue the conquest of the same coast and land, as he seemed to know something about navigation. The Friar passed this on to the Viceroy, and with the latter's permission is said to have gone overland in search of the same coast and country which I had discovered, and which was and is part of my *conquista*. And after his return, the Friar is said to have claimed he had gone so far as to see the said country. I deny that he could have seen or discovered it; but rather, what the Friar claims to have seen he had from me and was simply repeating what I had told him about the Indians of the said country of Santa Cruz.' Ycazbalceta, *Colección de Documentos para la Historia de Mexico*, Vol. II. Introduction, p.xxviii.

Developments back in Spain itself before even Friar Marcos set out, were to have an important effect on the race to find the Seven Cities. When Cabeza de Vaca reached Spain in the late summer of 1537, he learned to his intense disappointment that the command he aspired to had already gone to another. In the previous April, the Emperor had nominated Don Hernando de Soto as Governor of Cuba and Adelantado of Florida[1] with full rights of exploration, conquest, and settlement in the vast regions loosely designated by that name.

De Soto had made a name for himself and a fabulous fortune (from which the Emperor himself was not too proud to borrow) in the conquest of Peru. He had served his apprenticeship in arms in Darien under the grim old conquistador Pedrarias, whose daughter he had married, and he had then followed his comrade-in-arms Pizarro to Peru. De Soto had been the first Spanish envoy to Atahualpa, and though he had personally opposed the decision to put the Inca to death, he had benefited liberally from the division of his golden ransom. After serving for a time as Pizarro's lieutenant in Cuzco, he had returned to Spain before the outbreak of the calamitous civil wars amongst the conquistadores of Peru. His military fame, his wealth, his bold and ambitious spirit, clearly marked him out for further command. His appointment as Adelantado of Florida seemed to offer him scope for some brilliant achievements.

The new Adelantado was anxious to enrol Cabeza de Vaca in his expedition, for he saw the advantages of his unique experience of the country and understanding of its inhabitants. But Cabeza de Vaca firmly declined all de Soto's offers. Probably he realized how deeply he and de Soto differed in their conception of how a conquista should proceed, and above all in their attitude towards the

[1] Adelantado was the title generally given to the Governor of an unsettled or vaguely determined frontier zone.

Indians. Moreover, he wanted an independent command of his own.[1] The Emperor, though powerless to rescind the commission granted to de Soto, accorded Cabeza de Vaca the honour of a long private audience. Whatever secrets Cabeza de Vaca may have had for his royal master's ears are not known, but extravagant rumours were soon current throughout the Court. The Marquis of Astorga, who claimed to be in the know, sent a messenger post-haste to his brother and two kinsmen urging them to join de Soto's expedition without delay as it was sure to make their fortunes. Two of Cabeza de Vaca's own relatives sold all their possessions and also enlisted.

To the world at large, Cabeza de Vaca preserved a reticence which some said was but a ruse to keep from others the benefit of secrets which he was unable to turn to his own advantage. Others declared that he had made a pact with his comrade Dorantes to divulge nothing until they were able to return together to reap the golden harvest. But Dorantes had now abandoned his dreams for the solid comfort of his estate and well-to-do wife.

It only remained now for Hernando de Soto and the brilliant company he was busy assembling to reach the goal before his most important rival – the Viceroy of New Spain. By the autumn of 1538 de Soto had reached Havana, which was to be the base for his operations in Florida. There he learned of the preparations the Viceroy was making for further discoveries on the mainland. He at once dispatched an emissary to the Viceroy with copies of the commission he had been granted by the Emperor, and an implied warning that there was to be no poaching on his preserves. Mendoza sent a conciliatory answer professing pleasure at de Soto's coming and assuring him that there could be no clash of interests. In reality, the Viceroy was deeply alarmed.

---

[1] He was later appointed Governor of the Río de la Plata but his enlightened rule was nullified by the opposition of the turbulent and self-seeking soldiery, and he was forced to return to Spain.

To keep news of any discoveries which might be made by his people from reaching Cuba, he issued a proclamation that no one was to leave Mexico without his express permission. He need, as matters turned out, have had no fear. By the time the sensational first reports of the finding of the Seven Cities reached Cuba, de Soto was inextricably immersed in the Florida wilderness.

CHAPTER VI

De Soto makes his bid

The army which landed on the coast of Florida, at the end of May 1539, was one of the most formidable ever dispatched to the New World. 'Never before nor since in any other expedition for the conquest of the Indies,' declares Inca Garcilaso de la Vega, the mestizo author of a famous history of the conquest of Peru and of a highly coloured albeit second-hand account of de Soto's adventures in Florida, 'has such a goodly throng of people and horses been assembled together in a single force.' Accounts vary as to its exact strength, but it seems to have numbered at least six hundred officers and fighting men – far more, certainly, than the bands which sufficed to overthrow the Aztec and Inca empires. It was commanded by notable captains like the Comptroller Juan de Añasco, who prided himself on his skill as navigator and cosmographer no less than on his prowess as a soldier; Baltasar de Gallegos, a kinsman of Cabeza de Vaca who sold his possessions in order to take part in the venture; Luís Moscoso de Alvarado, the ruthless *maestre de campo* who was to lead back the remnants of the army after his General's death; the Treasurer Juan Gaitán, nephew of the powerful Cardinal de Siguenza and of an eponymous hero whose exploits gave rise to a proverbial phrase in the Spanish language – 'the sword and cape of Juan Gaitán'. As his second-in-command, de Soto had originally chosen Nuño de Tovar, a comrade-in-arms from Peru, but this officer had incurred the anger, and perhaps the jealousy, of his chief by seducing the seventeen-year-old daughter of the Count of Gomara, who had joined the expedition at the Canary Islands as Lady-in-waiting to Doña Isabel, de Soto's wife. Although the offender made amends by marrying the girl, he never managed to regain the favour of his General, who nominated a wealthy Cuban landowner, Porcallo de Figueroa, in his place. It was an unfortunate appointment. Porcallo de Figueroa's main interest in the venture was to acquire slaves for his estates, and although he enriched the expedition with ample supplies and equipment, he unashamedly abandoned it the moment he realized how dearly the savages of Florida would sell their freedom.

The rank and file of the expedition were drawn from many parts of the Emperor's wide domains, and even from lands beyond. A particularly large and well-armed contingent came from Portugal, and it is to one of these Portuguese adventurers, known as the Gentleman of Elvas, that we owe the most circumstantial first-hand account of the expedition.[1] Amongst volunteers of other nationality we find mention of a French priest from Paris, Biscayan carpenters, a Genoa master-craftsman who could construct anything from a bridge to a brigantine, a Spaniard reared in England, and even an unnamed Englishman whose skill with the long-bow matched that of the Indians. In addition to the fighting-men, there were a few women, numerous native servants and negro slaves, more than two hundred horses, and a pack of ferocious mastiffs trained to track down, guard, or tear recalcitrant Indians to pieces. A herd of swine – possibly the ancestors of the razor-backs of the south-west today – were taken along to serve as a reserve of pork rations.

De Soto opened operations by sending Captain Juan de Añasco to reconnoitre the coast of Florida for a harbour

---

[1] Published anonymously by the Gentleman of Elvas (translation in F. W. Hodge: *Spanish Explorers in the South United States, 1525-1543*). Other accounts of the expedition are by Ranjel, de Soto's secretary, in Oviedo's *Historia General y Natural de las Indias*, and by Biedma, the Factor of the expedition, in *Colección de Varios Documentos para la Historia de la Florida*, ed. Buckingham Smith (1857).

where the main expedition could disembark. The Comptroller returned without discovering anything suitable, and de Soto was obliged to make his landfall somewhere in the capacious, many-armed Bahía del Espíritu Santo, now known as Tampa Bay, which had been the starting point for the ill-fated Narváez expedition eleven years before. The Spaniards were in jubilant mood. Juan de Añasco had managed to kidnap a couple of savages from whose outlandish speech and vague signs they hopefully deduced the proximity of abundant gold. The soldiers boasted that their General had once helped to win the hoarded wealth of the Incas and would now surely lead them to still more fabulous treasure. They saw before them a virgin land, lush and sweet-scented in its spring freshness. The first to land returned with armfuls of rich grass for the exhausted horses and clusters of wild grapes for their comrades. Florida seemed a promised land indeed.

It was not until some days later that the first Indians were encountered. Amongst them was a man, all but indistinguishable from the natives, whom the Spaniards almost rode down. Luckily for himself and his rescuers, he was spared just in time on account of the few disjointed words of Castillian which he called out. It was Juan Ortiz, the sailor who had fallen into the hands of the Indians eleven years before when serving with the Narváez expedition, and who had survived by turning native. The adhesion of this man to de Soto's forces proved to be an event of major importance. Now, for the first time, the Spaniards could count on a trustworthy interpreter familiar with the language and mentality of the Florida Indians.

Through Ortiz, de Soto was able to establish contact with Mucozo, the chieftain who had befriended him. After bestowing gifts of clothes, weapons, and a fine horse, de Soto came briskly to the point and asked whether Mucozo had knowledge of any land where gold and silver were to be found. The Indian replied simply that he knew nothing of such things, as he had never ventured further than a dozen leagues from his dwelling place; but some thirty leagues off, he added, there lived a more powerful chief called Paracoxi in a land of rich maize-fields. De Soto forthwith despatched a captain to seek him out. But Paracoxi, though professing friendship, was distrustful of the Spaniards and went into hiding. His messengers told the Spaniards that they could find what they were seeking to the west, at a place called Cale, 'where summer reigned for most of the year, and men wore golden hats like helmets'. A number of Paracoxi's men, in token of friendship and in hope of plunder, offered to accompany the Spaniards.

To Cale, then, de Soto decided to march. A garrison of one hundred men was left behind as a base, and a small ship sent back to convey Porcallo de Figueroa, already disillusioned with the prospects of Florida as a slave reserve, to Cuba. The hardships of the campaign now began in grim earnest. The trail which the Spaniards followed led across a marsh, which the foot soldiers crossed by a makeshift bridge and the horses with the help of a hawser. Food was short. Water-cress and palmetto leaves were poor sustenance for men on the march, and even the maize they had found at Cale was a mean substitute for the gold they had looked for. Since few Indians had been captured, the Spaniards had to attend to their own needs themselves, pounding the maize laboriously in mortars of hollowed log with the help of wooden pestles, and then sifting the flour through their shirts of mail, or munching the parched grains whole when they lacked the patience for this labour. But visions of ease and plenty beckoned them on; in Apalache, the natives assured them, they would find everything they desired.

Before leaving Cale, the Spaniards suffered a loss which, though trivial in itself, throws light on the scale of values prevailing amongst the conquistadores and was deeply lamented throughout the army. Bruto, the most redoubtable and sagacious of their mastiffs, fell a victim to Indian arrows. The incident occurred when a force of hostile braves suddenly appeared on the further bank of a river which the Spaniards were preparing to cross. Before his masters could hold him back, Bruto broke away from the page who held his leash and made straight for the enemy. The stream was broad and swift, and the animal's head presented an easy target for the Indian marksmen. He succeeded in reaching the far side only to fall dead as he struggled from the water, his head and shoulders pierced, so Garcilaso declares, by more than fifty arrows. Thus did Bruto join the shades of Ponce de León's Becerillo and the latter's Leoncillo, who won for his master Balboa more than two thousand pesos of gold as his share of plunder, in the Valhalla of the Spaniards' war-dogs.

As the army toiled across the water-logged wilderness towards Apalache, the soldiers became aware that they were heading for regions through which, like the men of Narváez, they might be unable to force a path. Some began to murmur that they should turn back while there was yet time. But de Soto was inflexible, refusing to admit that what others found impossible would be impossible for him. Meanwhile, there were more immediate dangers to face. The natives were professing friendship, but de Soto suspected treachery, especially when they began to assemble powerful forces on the pretext that they had come to honour the strangers by staging a ceremonial parade. The Spaniards resolved to strike first, and fell upon them in a stretch of open country bounded by two lakes. The Indians, taken by surprise, could offer little resistance. More than three hundred of them were run down and lanced, a few managed to escape into the forests, while the rest sought safety in the lakes. Grimly the Spaniards posted themselves around the water and tried to shoot down the fugitives with cross-bows and arquebus. Cold and exhaustion at length forced the Indians to make for the shore under cover of darkness,

their heads camouflaged with the leaves of aquatic plants.
But the horsemen were waiting for them, and would charge
into the water, forcing the Indians to give themselves up or
turn back. Juan Ortiz called to them loudly in the Indian
tongue, bidding them come forth if they would save their
lives. One after another, the braves struggled from the water
and gave themselves up, until only a dozen or so, the
strongest and most stubborn, remained in the water. Finally,
de Soto ordered his native auxiliaries to plunge in after them.
The last of the enemy were dragged out by the hair, more
dead than alive, put into chains, and divided up amongst
their captors with the rest. Garcilaso says that, as a result of
this battle and the trapping of the Indians in the lakes,
more than nine hundred fell captive to the Spaniards.

But these warlike savages were not the stuff of which
slaves could be made, and they soon turned on their captors.
One day, when the Spaniards had just finished eating, the
captive chieftain who had been seated beside de Soto 'rose
to his feet with all conceivable savagery and ferocity and
closed at once with the Adelantado. Seizing him by the
collar with his left hand, he gave him such a blow over the
eyes, mouth and nose with his right fist that he knocked
down the chair in which he was seated and stretched him
out senseless on his back as if he had been a child. Then, to
finish off his victim, he let himself fall upon him, whilst at
the same time giving such a tremendous roar that it could
be heard a quarter of a league around.' This roar was the
signal for the other captives to set upon their masters
throughout the camp. 'As weapons, they made use of the
burning wood from the fire or other things found at hand;
many struck their masters in the face and burned them
with pots of boiling food, others struck them with plates,
crocks, jars, and pitchers, whilst others again used chairs,
benches, and tables if they were to be had, and if not, anything else that came to hand.' But the revolt of the fettered
savages – as desperate a piece of tragic slapstick as can be

found in the annals of the Conquista – could end only in one way. Their bruised and resentful masters restored order and sent the captives off to execution. Those who were not struck down at once were bound to stakes and then shot to death by the Indians whom the Spaniards had brought along with them from the friendly tribe of Paracoxi.

It was now the end of October, and the army pushed on through swamps and lurking Indian ambushes towards Apalache. They were approaching a fertile country, with numerous settlements and plantations of maize and beans. Here Narváez had quartered his army and sought in vain for the rumoured hoards of gold. The coast was only some ten leagues away, but the maze of creeks and marsh land which fringed it thwarted the attempts of reconnaissance parties to break through to the open sea. At length they reached a lagoon on the shores of which were traces of an abandoned camp. Heaps of charcoal ashes marked the spot where a forge had once been built, and the ground was strewn with the skulls of horses. The Spaniards had reached the Bahía de los Caballos, where Narváez had built his brigantines and the cavalry had sacrificed their mounts. De Soto's men scanned the trunks of the trees for any messages which their predecessors might have left, but nothing was found. Further down the shores of the lagoon, a search party came upon some disused canoes in which they put out to take soundings. The water was just deep enough, it seemed to them, to take larger vessels. With this report they returned to the General who decided that the time was now ripe to order the evacuation of the garrison which he had left behind at Tampa Bay where his expedition had first landed.

The difficult task of returning overland to Tampa Bay, through regions where the Indians would be quick to take up arms against their old enemies, was entrusted to the Comptroller, Juan de Añasco, and a picked band of horsemen. Añasco covered the distance without major mishap in ten days, despatched two of the caravels to Cuba with a small cargo of female slaves captured on the way, sent back the cavalry and a few crossbowmen by the overland route whilst he embarked the rest of the foot-soldiers and set off coasting down the peninsular until he should reach a safe anchorage within easy reach of Apalache. De Soto had ordered the rendezvous to be well marked by flags and on reaching it, Añasco turned over command of the brigantines to a captain of infantry called Diego Maldonado and re-joined de Soto's headquarters. Maldonado's orders were to sail on down the coast until finding a first-class harbour. Two months later he returned with the news that he had discovered an excellent anchorage, sheltered from all winds and with enough draft to take the largest vessels. The Indians called the place Ochus or Achusi; it was probably the fine land-locked Pensacola Bay, some two hundred miles west of the base of the Florida peninsula. In confirmation of his report, Maldonado brought back a couple of kid-napped natives, one of them a local chieftain.

This was heartening news indeed. Here at last was the prospect of a secure base for sea communications with Cuba and for regular colonization and exploration inland. The General ordered the brigantines to sail to Cuba with the good tidings and then to return with fresh supplies and reinforcements to await him at Ochus, which he proposed to reach after making a great sweep inland in order to probe the interior for gold. A couple of Indian youths brought in by a raiding party whilst the army was wintering at Apalache, had already reawakened expectations. They spoke of a land to the east 'governed by a lady, the town where she resided being of astonishing size and having many lands as her tributaries, some of whom rendered her clothing, others gold in quantity'. One of the youths pointed to a pearl which a Spaniard was wearing and vowed that the country was rich in such things, as well as in gold, and 'showed how the metal was taken from the earth, melted and refined, just as if he had seen it all done – or else the Devil had taught him how it was done'. The Spaniards who listened to him declared that no Indian could have described such things unless he had witnessed them with his own eyes.

At the beginning of March, the army left their winter quarters at Apalache and resumed the march. For many days they struggled through a pathless wilderness until hunger pressed upon them so sorely that the General gave orders that some of his precious swine should be slaughtered, and the friendly Indians who had attached themselves to the army were forced to disperse as there was no longer sufficient food for them. As for the two Indian guides with their tales of a great Queen and her stores of gold and pearls, the Spaniards threatened to throw them to the dogs, and would have done so had there been other guides with whom Juan Ortiz could understand and converse. At last a mean settlement, with a small stock of maize, was reached. The inhabitants were sullen and uncommunicative. It was only when de Soto had one of them burnt alive to encourage the others to talk that they admitted knowledge of a rich neighbouring land. It was called Cutifachique, and it was indeed blessed with gold and pearls and ruled by a woman, as the two youths had said.

De Soto lost no time in dispatching messengers to announce his approach and offer friendship to the Lady of Cutifachique. When the Spaniards reached the banks of a river, which evidently marked the borders of her domain, emissaries came out with tidings that their mistress herself was on her way to greet them. Soon the lady appeared, borne in her state canoe 'over the stern of which was stretched an awning, whilst on the bottom a mat was spread, with two cushions, one placed above the other, on which she sat', whilst her chief men accompanied her in other canoes. An extraordinary scene, this meeting of chieftainess and conquistador in the heart of the wilderness – 'less spectacular in grandeur and majesty, indeed, but like unto the manner in which Cleopatra went forth to receive Mark Anthony', declares the Inca Garcilaso, who extols her royal and dignified bearing, the elegance and discretion of her speech, and 'her great beauty, which was courtly in the extreme'. Other accounts confirm that she was young and well disposed towards the strangers. One chronicler contents himself with observing that she was 'dusky but well-proportioned'.

The Lady of Cutifachique presented the Spaniards with gifts of skins and clothing, and as she addressed them, she 'unwound little by little a large strand of pearls as thick as hazelnuts which encircled her neck thrice and fell to her thighs'. This she offered in token of friendship to the General, who responded by removing from his own finger and presenting a gold ring set with rubies. A fleet of canoes and rafts was then assembled to convey the Spaniards across the river, some of them taking up quarters in the half of a large village which the natives had vacated for them, whilst others camped in booths and arbours made for them by the Indians beneath the shade of mulberry and walnut trees. Maize and turkeys were brought to them, and brilliantly hued clothing fashioned from feathers and the bark of trees. But when the Lady of Cutifachique learned from the Spaniards that of all her gifts those they prized most were the pearls, she bade them go to the sacred places where her ancestors were buried, for there they would find as many pearls as they wished.

One such temple or burial place stood in the village where the Spaniards were quartered. When the General and his officers entered it they found a scene of gruesome splendour. Round the walls were ranged open chests and cane baskets filled to the brim with pearls, and on these thrones, or on piles of furs and hides, reposed the decaying bodies of the dead. De Soto seized a couple of handfuls of pearls and told his companions to do likewise; they would serve very well, he declared, for rosaries. Some were for carrying off great loads of the pearls, there and then. But de Soto dissuaded them, urging that they still had far to go and that better things would fall to their lot.

A league or so away stood a larger town, the residence and royal burial place of the rulers of Cutifachique. The Spaniards found the place all but deserted, for a recent pestilence had driven the people from their homes. In the middle of the town stood the temple – a large structure – more than a hundred feet long and forty wide, if we are to believe the Inca Garcilaso. Its roof was made of reeds plastered over with patterns of sea-shells and pearls, some of which drooped to the ground in gleaming strands like icicles. Large wooden figures flanked the entrance, brandishing clubs, spears, and wooden-bladed swords, as if to guard the place from desecration. Inside were ranged the coffins of the chieftains, each surmounted by an effigy of the dead man, whilst the walls above them were hung with round or oval shields of cane adorned with pearls and coloured fringes. A number of smaller alcoves, like chapels, led off from the main hall, where piles of weapons of every sort were stacked, so that the place had the appearance of an arsenal as much as a temple. The pearls, which were the object of the Spaniards' quest, were kept in wooden chests in the nave, or central part of the building; line after line of them, chest stacked on chest, in tapering piles, to form dazzling pyramids of treasure. The Spaniards gazed at the sight incredulously. Some were for ransacking the temple there and then, but de Soto once more restrained them. How could such booty be borne through the swamps and forests of Florida back to Cuba? If God willed, they would return before long to reap the strange harvest.

Many of the Spaniards, seeing the fertility of the land, the wealth of pearls which it contained, and the friendliness of the natives and their mistress, held that they should stay and found a settlement. But de Soto would not listen. There was not sustenance enough in the land for the whole army, he declared; nor were the pearls, for all their vast number, a sufficient treasure, for they had been flawed through being extracted by fire. What they had seen here should serve only to whet their appetite. The General was resolved, so the Portuguese chronicler declares, 'to find another treasure like that of Atahualpa, Lord of Peru, and would not be content with good lands nor pearls'. Moreover, he had ordered the brigantines to return with fresh supplies from Cuba and await him at Ochus. The march to Cutifachique had brought them a good two hundred and fifty miles north of Apalache, probably to the region of the Savannah River, in present-day South Carolina. De Soto, it seems, was now only a few days' march from the Atlantic, not far from the coast where the Licentiate Ayllón had landed and met his end, for a few metal objects of obviously Spanish origin had found their way into the possession of the Cutifachique Indians. But since their General was 'an inflexible man, dry of word, who did not like to be contradicted once he had said a thing', the Spaniards regretfully abandoned the idea of founding a colony and prepared to leave Cutifachique.

For the manner of their leaving, we must take our choice of two rather different accounts. Garcilaso assures us that de Soto 'took leave of the Indian mistress of Cutifachique and the principal people of her town, thanking them profusely for the courtesy shown him in their land, thus leaving them as friends and warm admirers of the Spaniards'. The Gentleman of Elvas is more cynical. The chieftainess, he asserts, was placed under guard and made to march along with the army until she at last managed to give them the slip and conceal herself in the forest. The Spaniards were piqued at her escape as she carried with her a bag of unbored pearls, whose value was held to be far greater than those of the temple hoards. But they never managed to recapture her and it was later reported that she returned safely to her own people where she was making amends for her misadventures by living with an escaped slave of one of the

An Indian medicine man performs his rites.

Building a wooden fort in Florida.

Spaniards. Such, in all probability, was the unromantic end of the Antony and Cleopatra episode of de Soto's expedition.

Instead of striking a new course to the south-west, in the general direction of Ochus and the Gulf of Mexico, de Soto chose to cross the Savannah River and march first to the north and then to the north-east, in search of new lands and treasure, sweeping through the southernmost tip of what is now North Carolina and South Tennessee, before swinging southwards in an immense arc towards Ochus. For the greater part of the trek, the natives proved friendly, or at least could be cowed into submission without difficulty, for they were less warlike than the savages of the coast. The demands of the Spaniards seldom varied; food for themselves and their mounts, bearers and sometimes a contingent of slaves. The local chiefs were always summoned and compelled to accompany the army to the borders of their tribal territory. And always, too, there was the eternal questing and questioning for gold.

After many weeks' arduous march, the Spaniards entered the territory of a powerful chief called Tascaluza. He received the strangers seated in state beneath a standard of painted deerskin, with his warriors ranged in a wide semi-circle around him. Tascaluza was an impressive figure, 'tall of person, muscular, lean, and well-proportioned – the suzerain of many territories and of a numerous people, being feared by his vassals and by neighbouring tribes alike'. De Soto treated him with a show of deference, and gave him a horse to ride, though it was not easy to find a mount able to bear the exceptional weight of the man. Tascaluza accompanied the army some way in its southward march, but showed no signs of being overawed by the Spaniards. He sent out messengers ostensibly with orders that his subjects should get ready supplies for the strangers, but it was suspected that he was secretly bidding them prepare for battle. The Spaniards came at length to a settlement called Mavilla ruled by a vassal of Tascaluza. The place contained some eighty houses, each large enough to accommodate several households and to serve as strongholds in case of need. It was surrounded by a stout palisade of beams and hardened mud and stood in the middle of a broad plain. As the Spaniards approached, escorted by Tascaluza riding his sturdy horse and resplendent in a scarlet cloak given him by the General, a troop of dancing girls and musicians came out to receive them. The women of this tribe were comely, and Luís de Moscoso later took one back as a slave to Mexico where he delighted in showing off her good looks.

De Soto drew up the main body of his army on the plain and entered Mavilla with a dozen of his own guards and officers. Tascaluza invited him to quarter his suite in one of the large houses which had been prepared for their reception. Tascaluza then entered another house where his war-chiefs were assembled, and once in their company refused to come out to rejoin the Spaniards. Whether the Indians were already resolved to attack is not certain. Their immediate aim seems to have been to prevent the Spaniards keeping Tascaluza in their power, for the Gentleman of Elvas says that he replied to all de Soto's messages by saying 'he would not come forth or leave that town; that if the Governor wished to go in peace, he should leave at once, and not strive to carry him away from his own country'. The situation grew tense, the Spaniards demanding that the chief return to them, Tascaluza bidding defiance from the midst of his braves. Baltasar de Gallegos, who had accompanied de Soto, seized hold of a chief and made as if to send him by force to fetch his master out. The Indian slipped free and reached to fit an arrow to his bow. Baltasar swiftly cut him down with his sword. Battle was joined.

The handful of Spaniards who had entered the palisaded settlement now found themselves trapped. Shouting to his men to follow, de Soto fought his way to the gate. Five of his suite were killed and he himself struck to the ground three or four times before he reached the open plain. Two priests, a page, and a slave woman, who found themselves cut off, barricaded themselves inside one of the houses and held out until eventually rescued in the Spaniards' general assault on the town. The Indians pursued de Soto and his companions out into the plain and then set free the great train of Indian carriers and prisoners whom they brought into the settlement, with all the Spaniards' baggage, and hastily armed them against their masters. The main force of the Spaniards was slow to rally, for some had tethered their horses near the town and had no time to free them before the Indians started to loose off their arrows. Others, with no thought of impending danger, still lingered in the rear and did not come up until the heat of the battle was over.

When the Spaniards had recovered from the shock of the Indians' initial onslaught, de Soto grouped his men into four strong infantry detachments and advanced against the palisade. Some horsemen remained in the plain to strike down any Indians who might break out. Once the Spaniards had forced their way back into Mavilla, the order was given to set fire to the wooden houses. The Indians who escaped the swords of the Spaniards found death in the flames or beneath the spears of the waiting horsemen. The carnage was remorseless. By nightfall, after the fiercest battle which they had fought since landing in Florida, the Spaniards could claim the total destruction of the enemy. The body of chief Tascaluza, with hundreds of his braves, lay beneath the smouldering ruins of Mavilla. But for the Spaniards it was a pyrrhic victory. Accounts of their losses vary from eighteen to forty-seven dead. Few escaped without wounds and many died later from their effects. Scarcely less serious for the fighting power and morale of the army was the loss of some forty-five horses, such medical and food supplies as the Spaniards had with them, and their entire equipment, including the pearls of Cutifachique, the wine reserved for the celebration of mass, and the packs of playing cards for the gambling which was the men's favourite pastime – each loss, for its own reason, bitterly lamented.

The disastrous battle of Mavilla marks the turning point in de Soto's fortunes. He had brought his army, without serious loss, to within a dozen miles of Ochus harbour, where the brigantines were waiting for him with supplies from Cuba. It only remained for him to march on to the coast and to use his fresh resources for establishing a permanent base at this excellent natural port. But Mavilla spoiled all. It showed that the coastal Indians were too warlike and too treacherous ever to submit and serve the Christians willingly. Most of the pearls of Cutifachique had vanished in the smoke and flames of battle, and with them the only tangible evidence of the riches to be found in the new land. The morale of the army had been shattered. The ragged and famished soldiers, shivering in huts improvised round the ashes of Mavilla, now had only one thought; to fill their bellies and heal their wounds in a Christian land. Even the most valiant captains like Juan Gaitán talked openly of abandoning the expedition and sailing back to Cuba as soon as they reached the brigantines. De Soto, prowling anxiously round the camp at night, knew of these murmurings, and a fatal and inflexible decision formed in his mind. He would turn his back on the waiting ships and give the faint-hearts no chance to desert. They would march again through the vast and hostile wilderness of the interior in quest of the prizes which he still stubbornly believed that Providence held in store. So the momentous resolve was taken to let the brigantines sail back to Cuba alone; 'the source and principal cause of the ruination of this cavalier and his whole army,' writes the Inca Garcilaso, with an insight for once unclouded by courtly sentiment, 'for from that day on, as one frustrated, whose own people had played his hopes false and barred the way to his good desires and nullified the plan he had made for settling and perpetuating the land, he never managed to do anything to his advantage, nor indeed does it seem he so much as tried. But rather, instigated by disdain, he continued from that time on until he died, squandering both time and life to no avail, and for ever journeying from one place to another without rhyme or reason, as one who abhorred life and, as we shall see, desired to bring it to an end.'

With every allowance made for the pride and obstinacy of their leader, the action of the Spaniards in turning back again into the wilderness after Mavilla still remains largely inexplicable unless we assume a factor for which there is only indirect evidence in the contemporary chronicles. Common prudence would have demanded that the General should at least make contact with the brigantines to collect the supplies which his men so badly needed. But there is no reason to suppose that he did so. He was bent, it seems, on preventing even this measure of contact. We only know that, sometime before the battle, messengers reached him to report the ships' arrival. They must have brought him, too, his first news of the outside world for sixteen months, and there can be little doubt as to what the highlights of that news must have been. So great had been the stir made in Cuba by reports emanating from New Spain, and such was the importance which de Soto's officials in that island attached to them for the success of their master's expedition, that those who seemed to know most were required to relate all they knew under oath. These sworn statements have survived[1] and show that by November 1539 rumours were current in Cuba that, somewhere to the north of Mexico, there had been discovered those lands of fabled wealth at which Cabeza de Vaca had hinted and which de Soto had set out to find – discovered, but not indeed yet conquered.

The name of this El Dorado was Cíbola. According to one of the witnesses, García Navarro, it was 'a land rich in gold, silver and other wealth, and has great cities; the houses are

[1] Quoted in *Coronado; Knight of Pueblos and Plains*, by H. E. Bolton, pp. 50-52.

of stone and terraced like those of Mexico; the people have weights and measures, and are civilized. They marry only once, wear woollen clothes, and ride about on some animals whose name the witness does not know.' Another witness added that the people of Cíbola spoke the Aztec tongue and were ruled by Kings. A third man, by name Andres García, related that Cíbola had actually been glimpsed by an adventurous friar who had then returned to Mexico and reported all about it not only to the Viceroy but even to the son of the witness, who happened to be a barber and had the news from the friar himself whilst the latter was being shaved. The barber learned from him that the people of Cíbola dwelt in walled cities and that they were so rich that the women wore belts made of gold. All this, and more, was already so much common knowledge in Mexico that the Viceroy had set about raising a great force for the immediate conquest of the new lands.

Such was the dramatic news reaching Cuba and which de Soto was now hearing for the first time. But what in fact had Friar Marcos really discovered?

CHAPTER VII

Friar Marcos views the Promised Land

In March 1539 – two months before de Soto set sail from Havana for Florida – Friar Marcos, with the viceregal commission in his baggage, left Culiacán on his long trek to the north. He was accompanied by Brother Onorato, a Franciscan lay-brother and fellow-Savoyard, the Negro Esteban, and the Indians who had once escorted Cabeza de Vaca and who had then been kept in Mexico City for a time to grow familiar with Spanish ways and the Christian faith. Reassured by the presence of their fellow tribesmen and the gentle words and ways of the friars, the Indians of the border-lands came out to welcome them as friends.

The trail which the Friar followed lay between the Gulf of California and the great chain of the Sierra Madre mountains. This long wedge-shaped tract of land was traversed at intervals by rivers flowing down from the hills – first, the Petatlán River, now known as Río del Fuente, which marked the boundary between the province of Sinaloa, with Culiacán as its centre, and the less known country to the north which the Spaniards called Señora and the Indians (bequeathing the name in use today) Sonora. Parallel to the Petatlán, and separated by miles of rugged land, flowed two other rivers, the Mayo and the Yaqui, which take their names from the tribes dwelling on their banks. Beyond these again was the Sonora River, along whose marvellously fertile upper valley an ancient Indian trail led inland to the deserts and vast plains of the interior. From river to river, skirting the great mountain chain and thus edging away from coast as it gradually veered to the north-east, the Friar and his party made their slow way towards the pass at the head of the Sonora valley.

After an initial set-back at Petatlán, where Friar Onorato fell sick and had to be sent back, everything went well. As they passed through the native settlements, many Indians attached themselves to the party, as they had once done to Cabeza de Vaca and his companions whose memory was still cherished amongst them. The Negro was a spectacular link between the two ventures. Estebán took obvious delight in the rôle he was now called upon to play. Bells jingled merrily from his arms and ankles, two large greyhounds escorted him, and Indian servants carried the magic gourd, adorned with bells and coloured feathers, which had served him so well as a symbol of his sacred office.

The trail led at first within easy reach of the sea. 'I saw nothing worthy of note here,' the Friar reported, in his dispatch to the Viceroy, 'except that there came to me Indians from the island in which the Marqués del Valle [Cortés] had been.' The Friar showed them some pearls from the samples of various metals and other goods which he carried with him, and the Indians told him that there were many such things to be found on their island home. A four days' march across desert country brought Friar Marcos to the next tribe who came out in amazement to gape at the strangers, for they had never seen a white man before. 'They called me Sayola,' he relates, 'which means in their tongue the Man from the Sky.' These Indians probably belonged to the warlike Yaqui tribe. The Friar showed them further samples from his bag and they pointed to the gold and told him that four or five days' march inland, towards the mountains, they would find a large valley inhabited by folk who dressed in cotton and wore nose and ear ornaments of the same metal.

This was heartening news, but the Friar could not let himself be diverted from his main quest. The coastal plains were now gradually broadening out as the gulf swung away from the line of the mountains. Friar Marcos kept on to the north, reaching at last a fair-sized settlement called Vacapa in fertile, well-watered country some forty leagues from the coast. The Friar had now been travelling for more than a month and had covered about five hundred miles. He rested in Vacapa while messengers were sent to the coast. They came back with reports that there were numerous islands inhabited by warlike Indians. Some of the latter returned with the messengers and attached themselves to the Friar's motley retinue, though they were traditional enemies of the people of Vacapa. But the Man from the Sky healed old feuds and seemed to unite friend and foe in a common loyalty to himself and to the sign of the Cross. The latter was an emblem familiar to the aborigines of America from their own rites. In the hands of the Friar it became a symbol of peace and friendship which they regarded as sacred.

In Vacapa, Friar Marcos made a momentous decision. Now that they must be nearing the country of the Seven Cities, it seemed to him best to send on Estebán in advance. It may well be that the negro had begun to cause trouble and that the restrained and pious tone of the Friar's dealings with the natives was not at all to his liking. His was a more flamboyant nature, and the obvious impression which he caused on the natives may have gone to his head. Marcos, in his dispatches, has no complaint to make of him, but if we are to believe the gossip reported by the chronicler Pedro de Castañeda[1] 'the negro did not get on well with the friars because he took the women that were given him and collected turquoises, and got together a stock of everything'. Whatever the reason may have been, Estebán was ordered to go on ahead with instructions, 'to go to the North fifty or sixty leagues, to see if in that direction there might be observed something great, or some country rich and well

[1] Hodge and Lewis, op. cit. p. 288.

settled; and if he found or heard of anything of that kind, to stop and send me a message by some Indians. That message was to consist of a wooden cross of white colour. In case the discovery was of fair importance, he was to send me a cross one span in length; if really important, the cross was to be two spans in length; and if something bigger and greater than New Spain, he should send me a large cross.'[1]

Four days later the first messengers arrived from the negro. To his amazement, Marcos saw that they were carrying a cross as large as a man. Could it be possible – a discovery of such rich promise – and only four days' march away! With the cross came a message urging the Friar to hurry for all he was worth, 'since he had met people who gave him information of the greatest country in the world, and that he was with Indians who had been there, of whom he sent me one; and this man told me so many things of the greatness of the country that I refused to believe it until I saw it myself or obtained further proof'.

Further proof, it seems, was soon forthcoming. Other Indians from a different tribe joined the Friar's party. They came from the east and told him that their people sometimes travelled to the Seven Cities. Their reports seemed to tally with what the Indian whom Estebán had sent continued to narrate. The picture painted by this Indian was indeed a dazzling one. 'He said that from where Estebán now was it was thirty days' march to the first city of the country, which was called Cíbola. He further affirms that and says that in this first province there are seven very large cities, all under one lord, with houses of stone and mortar, the smallest ones of two storeys and with a flat roof, and others of three or four storeys, and that of the lord with five, all placed together in order; and on the doorsills and lintels of the principal houses many figures of turquoise stones, of which he said there was a great abundance; and that the

[1] Bandelier, op. cit.

people of these cities are very well clothed; and many other particulars he told me, as well about these Seven Cities as of other provinces beyond, of which he said that each was more important than the Seven Cities. In order to find out how he came to know all this, I questioned him a great deal, and found him of very good understanding.'

The Seven Cities, more marvellous in their promise of wealth and fame than the Spaniards had even imagined, were then at hand! On hearing such tidings, the good Friar might well comment: 'I gave thanks to Our Lord.'

For the first time, from the lips of this unknown Indian, the Spaniards heard the name which was from then on to be coupled with the Seven Cities – Cíbola.[1] How great an empire might be denoted by this new name Friar Marcos had little time to enquire, for Esteban was impatiently urging him on. While the Friar tarried (for he was awaiting news from the coast), a second cross, as tall as the first, arrived with an even more frantic message from the negro. In the face of this fresh summons there could be no further delay, and Friar Marcos set out with his Indian escort to overtake the negro with all possible speed. Esteban had been expressly ordered to wait for the Friar should there be news of importance, but when, after three days, Marcos reached the village from which the negro had sent his first message, there was no sign of him. His eagerness had got the better of him and he had hurried on ahead. 'He thought he could get all the reputation and honour for himself,' observes Castañeda sardonically, 'and that if he should discover these settlements with such famous high houses on his own account, he would be considered bold and courageous.' The negro slave had become infected by his masters' craving for gold and glory.

Friar Marcos had now reached the valley of the Sonora River where he was welcomed by people of the peace-loving Opata tribe. They confirmed everything of which

[1] At least Friar Marcos construed it as Cíbola. See p. 143.

the negro had sent him word; Cíbola lay within thirty days' journey, the first of seven great cities, all built of great and lofty houses. They gave him news too of other and still mightier kingdoms beyond called Marata, Acus, and Totonteac. These places, they declared, they had visited 'in search of turquoises, cow-hides, and other objects'. They had much to tell him about those turquoises, for the people of those lands were described as wearing them, 'good and fine ones, hanging from their ears and nostrils, and they say there are many decorations made of turquoises in the principal doorways of Cíbola'. Marcos went on to report to the Viceroy that the Indians of Sonora told him that 'the mode of dress in Cíbola is a cotton shirt reaching to the ankle, with a button at the throat and a long cord hanging from it, and the sleeves of the shirts are of equal width from shoulders to wrist. . . . They say they also wear girdles of turquoises, and that over the shirts some wear very good mantles, others cow-skins, well-prepared, of which they say there are many in that country, and they hold them in great esteem; also, that the women are dressed like the men, and clothed from head to foot.' In proof of what they said, the natives showed Friar Marcos a number of well-tanned cow-skins which they said came from Cíbola. In return for these good tidings, the Friar let the natives bring out their sick to touch the hem of his gown, whilst he recited passages from the Gospel over them.

Crosses and messages from the exuberant negro continued to reach the Friar as he made his way up the fertile Sonora valley, whose inhabitants came out to bestow gifts upon him – gifts which included cowhides and turquoises in earnest of the riches to come. So vivid and detailed were the accounts which the natives gave him of the Seven Cities and the kingdoms beyond that he almost fancied he was treading their streets and mingling with their richly clad citizens. 'I had on a gown of gray cloth,' he wrote in his report to the Viceroy, 'which the Governor of New

Galicia, Francisco Vasquez de Coronado, had caused me to wear. The chief of this pueblo and other Indians touched the garment with their hands and told me that there was much of the same kind at Totonteac, and that the natives dressed in it. I laughed at their remark saying that it could not be—and that they probably wore only cotton mantles. But they said: "Do you think we do not realize that what you wear is different from our dress? Know that at Cíbola the houses are filled with the cloth which we wear; but at Totonteac there is a kind of small animal from which they take wherewith to manufacture what you have on your body." I was much astonished, having never heard anything like it before, and enquired of them further, and they said that the animals are of the size of the two Spanish greyhounds which Estebán had with him; also that there are many of them at Totonteac. I could not find out what sort of animals they were."[1]

In short, the Friar continued, 'Cíbola was as well known here as Mexico City is in New Spain, or Cuzco in Peru; and they described fully the shape of the houses, the arrangement of the villages, the streets and squares, like people who had been there often, and who obtained there, in return for their services, the objects of luxury and convenience which they possessed. I told them it could not be possible that the houses were of such a kind as they represented; and in order to give me to understand it, they took soil and ashes, poured water on them, and showed me how they placed the stones, and how they raised the structure, putting together mud and stone till it rose on high. I asked the men if the people had wings so as to ascend those storeys; but they laughed, and described to me a ladder, as well as I could have done it myself, and they

---

[1] This passage has caused some speculation. Could the Indians be referring to the vicuña or the guanaca, of which only fossilized remains have been found in that part of America? Or could they simply have meant the fur of the jack-rabbit or cony, which the natives skilfully plaited into strips to form blankets and mantles?

took a pole which they held in their hands to show that that was the height from storey to storey. . . . In Totonteac the houses are like those of Cíbola, but better and more numerous, and of such size that there is no end to it.'

The fertile Sonora valley at length gave place to a tract of uninhabited land. There was still no sign of the negro, but at intervals along the trail the Indians who were with him had left bowers in which the Friar could shelter. After four days Friar Marcos reached the settlement known to the Spaniards as Corazones, after the gift of six hundred deers' hearts[1] which the natives had once bestowed on Cabeza de Vaca and Dorantes. At this point in his narrative, the Friar inserts a statement which is distinctly puzzling. 'Here I learned that the sea-coast veers sharply to the west,' he writes, 'for up to the first uninhabited tract it constantly tended towards the north: and as this change of direction in the coast is of much importance, I wished to know about it. So I set out for it and saw clearly that in 35 degrees[2] it does veer west.' What are we to make of this claim? Did the Friar, obviously excited by the news of Cíbola, really make the four hundred miles detour over rugged country simply to check the Indians' reports on the nature of the sea-coast? The hypothesis is ruled out alone by the dates given for the subsequent stages of his narrative. We are forced to the conclusion that here, at least – as Cortés later charged in his formal indictment—the Friar was claiming as his own achievement what he merely had on hearsay. And if this story of his trek to the coast must be held to be a fabrication, were the Spaniards justified in believing everything he had to say about the wonders of Cíbola?[3]

[1] See p. 68.
[2] The Friar is seriously out in his reckoning. The coast of Sonora begins to veer W./N.W. in Latitude 31.
[3] One authority frankly dismisses the latter half of the Friar's report as a fabrication: 'It is my belief that Friar Marcos started out into the despoblado, the high grassy steppe country which begins in N. Sonora, but shortly after entering it he heard from an Indian who had been with Stephen [Estebán] of the latter's death at the hand of the Zuñis, and

The upper valley of the Sonora River was the last oasis before the great *despoblado*, or uninhabited region, beyond which, so the Indians said, lay the promised land of Cíbola. Here Marcos actually encountered an old man who claimed he was a citizen of Cíbola but was living as a refugee from his own country. He confirmed and amplified the reports which the Friar had already received. 'Cíbola,' he declared, 'is a great city, in which there are many people, streets and squares, and in some parts of the city there are very large houses, as high as eleven storeys, in which the principal men come together on certain days of the year.' 'They also say,' continued the Friar's despatch, 'that the houses are of stone and mortar, as others had already told me, and that the entrances and fronts of the chief buildings are of turquoises. He told me too that the others of the Seven Cities are like this one, and some of them larger, and that the principal one of all is Ahacus. He says that towards the south-east there is a kingdom called Marata, in which there used to be many and large settlements, all of which are of stone, many-storeyed houses, and that this kingdom was, and still is, at war with the lord of the Seven Cities, through which warfare the kingdom of Marata had declined greatly, although it still holds its own, and is at war with the others. And he also stated that towards the south-east lies the kingdom called Totonteac, which he describes as the largest in the world, the most populous, and the wealthiest. . . . He also said that there is another very large province and kingdom called Acus. There is also Ahacus, and that word (with aspiration) is the name of one of the Seven Cities, the largest of them all; whilst Acus (without aspiration) is a province by itself. He offered to go with me to Cíbola and beyond, if I would take him along.'

In the face of such a flood of detailed testimony, what

that then Friar Marcos returned precipitously southwards, without ever seeing the Zuñi country or climbing to the Colorado Plateau, having penetrated at most a very short distance into the modern State of Arizona.' – Carl Sauer, *The Road to Cíbola*, (1932), p. 28.

shadow of doubt could now remain about the wonders of Cíbola? The Indians were questioned and cross-questioned, and all agreed that the fugitive was speaking the absolute truth. The negro was already half way across the *despoblado*, with an escort of 300 carriers and companions. Even the Friar was now in a fever of impatience – 'for each day seemed a year to me, on account of my desire to see Cíbola.' The natives vied with each other in their anxiety to go with him; 'in order to serve me and because they thought they would return home rich.' The Friar selected a distinguished company of the chief men, who set out with him attired in ceremonial dress and wearing their necklaces of turquoise, and accompanied by a train of carriers bearing supplies. They said it would take fifteen days to cross the *despoblado*.

Marcos started off on the final stage of his journey on 9 May – two months after leaving Culiacán. From the head of the Sonora Valley, the party had to cross rough country, heading across the present Mexican-U.S. border and then descending due north along the valley of the San Pedro River, after which the trail veered north-east across the Colorado plateau, in the present State of Arizona. The negro had passed that way not many days before, and at night the Friar sheltered in the bowers which his Indians had built. There was no serious lack of food, or even of water, for ample supplies were carried and rations were supplemented by game. For thirteen days they travelled thus, without undue discomfort, until the Indians said that they must be within three or four days' march of the first city. The expedition seemed to be proceeding under the special favour of God.

Then suddenly and terribly came a dramatic reversal of fortune. One of Estebán's native escort was met flying for his life. He gasped out that when his companions had reached the city, the men of Cíbola had set upon the negro and killed him. Many of the escort had likewise perished.

The rest were on their way back in panic-stricken flight. Terror now seized the Indians of the Friar's entourage. Disaster had fallen so swiftly, so unexpectedly, that they could hardly believe it. They vowed they would go no further, and only with the greatest difficulty and by opening the packs he had given them to carry and distributing amongst them the contents which he had intended as gifts for Cíbola, could the Friar console them and prevail on them to proceed. When they were within about one day's journey from the city, they were met by another party of blood-stained fugitives. At this fresh evidence of disaster, the Indians set up a great wailing and weeping, in which Marcos himself could hardly refrain from joining. 'And such was the lamentation, that they did not let me ask after Estebán to learn what had happened, nor allow me to calm them. "How can we calm ourselves," they answered, "since we know our fathers and sons and brothers and more than three hundred men who went with Estebán, have been done to death?" And they vowed they no longer dared go to Cíbola as they had been wont.'

Only by degrees could the story be pieced together, and this is what the Friar learned: 'As Estebán arrived within a day's journey of Cíbola he sent his messengers to the lord of the place, informing him of his coming, and that he intended to treat for peace with him and cure the sick. When they gave the gourd to the chief, and he saw the rattles, he threw down the gourd in a rage and said: "I know these people, for these rattles are not of the same kind as our own. Tell them to turn back at once, else not one of them shall remain alive." So the messengers returned to Estebán in sorrow, hardly venturing to tell him. But at length they informed him of what had happened, and he said to them that they should not be afraid, that he would go there, for whenever the Indians, on his previous travels, gave him evil words at the outset, it was a sure sign that he would be well received by them. So he went forward and reached the city of Cíbola, about sundown, with all the people of his escort, of whom there were about three hundred men and many women. But they refused to let him into the city, and quartered him in a large and good house outside. Besides, they took away from Estebán all he carried, saying that the chief thus ordained it, and all that night they gave us neither to eat nor to drink. The next day, after the sun had risen to the height of a lance, Estebán went out of the house and some of the principal men of his escort with him. Forthwith there came many people from the city, and as soon as he saw them he fled, and we with him. Then it was that they gave us these wounds with their arrows, and we fell. Others fell on top of us, dead, and so we remained until night, afraid to move. We heard a great uproar in the city, and saw on the flat roofs many men and women who were looking; but we saw nothing of Estebán, and believe that he was killed with arrows, like the rest of those who came with him, and that we alone escaped.'

Castañeda, writing a few years later, gives some additional details to fill in the picture. 'For three days they made inquiries about him and held a council. The account which the negro gave them of two white men[1] who were following him, sent by a great lord, who knew about the things in the sky, and how these were coming to instruct them in divine matters, made them think that he must be a spy or a guide from some nations who wished to come and conquer them, because it seemed to them unreasonable to say that the people were white in the country from which he came, and that he was sent by them, he being black. Besides these other reasons, they resented his demanding from them turquoises and women, and so they decided to slay him.'

The memory of the negro's death is preserved to this day in local Indian legend. A 'black Mexican', one of the versions has it, once came journeying from the land of Everlasting Summer. He was a large man, with lips as red as

[1] Castañeda mistakenly assumes that Fr Onorato was still with the party.

chillies, and such were his greed and his insufferable preten-
sions that the wise men of the Indians decided to put him to
death. Another folk tale has it that they gave him a great
kick which sped him through the air back to the south
whence he had come.

But fact was more brutal than legend. Estebán was assuredly dead. The horrifying news, and the thought that
their own kinsmen had perished on his account, filled the
Indians escorting the Friar Marcos with consternation and
anger. They heaped reproaches on the head of the white
man and even threatened to take his life to atone for the
losses their tribe had suffered. To lead them on to Cíbola
after this tragedy was clearly out of the question. Yet the
prize was now so nearly within the Friar's grasp – or at least
within his view. Finally, by dint of much persuasion, Marcos
induced two of the chiefs who were with him to guide him
on to a place from which he could set eyes on the city. Then
at last the vision lay before him: 'We came within sight of
Cíbola,' he reported to the Viceroy, 'which lies on a plain
at the foot of a round hill. Its aspect is that of a very fine
place – the best I have seen in these parts. The houses are
just as the Indians had told me – all built of stone, with their
storeys and flat roofs, so far as I could tell from the eminence
which I climbed so as to view it. The settlement is greater
than the city of Mexico. At times I felt tempted to go on to
it, since I knew that I had only my life to risk, and this I had
offered to God the day I set out on the expedition. But I was
afraid, for I knew the danger I was in and that if I were to
die there would perish with me the knowledge of this land
which, in my view, is the greatest and best of all those yet
discovered.'

Yet what the Friar beheld must be only a small part of all
the wonders in store. His Indian guides kept assuring him
that Cíbola 'was the smallest of the Seven Cities, and that
Totonteac is far larger than all the seven put together, and
has so many houses and people that there is no end to it'.

What could be done to reap so vast a harvest? With the help of the Indians, the Friar heaped together a small pile of stones and placed a wooden cross upon it, 'slender and small, for I lacked the means of making a larger one', and named the newly-discovered land the New Kingdom of St Francis, announcing that he took possession, in the name of the Viceroy and his lord the Emperor, 'of all the Seven Cities, and of the Kingdoms of Totonteac, of Achus, and of Marata'. But, the Friar cautiously added, 'that I was not going forward to them, in order that I might report what had been seen and done.' The little ceremony hurriedly completed, he turned back to the lamenting Indians and together they set off with all possible speed on the long trek home, as he frankly confesses, 'with more fear than food'.

As they neared the frontiers of New Spain once more, Friar Marcos could thankfully feel that God had singled him out for special favour. Not only was he back safe and sound after his adventures, but the expedition had, all things considered, proved a brilliant success. The confidence of the friendly natives, it is true, had been rudely shaken. A vainglorious negro slave had lost his life. But the Seven Cities of Cíbola, and lands of still greater promise beyond, had been discovered. It now only remained for them to be conquered.

The Wilderness Wins

Was there still time to get to Cíbola first?

This was the question which tormented Hernán de Soto as he listened to news and rumours reaching him from Cuba. He had staked everything – wealth, reputation, life itself, and those of the hundreds entrusted to his leadership – on the success of this great gamble. Now he learned that the prize was within the grasp of a rival. The golden cities had actually been seen. No one could tell him exactly where, but they must surely lie somewhere amidst the vast unknown lands to the north – somewhere north of Florida, north of the great Gulf of Mexico, north of Pánuco, north of the outermost provinces of New Spain. Was there still time to reach Cíbola first? His men were exhausted, their supplies gone, and now, after Mavilla, their spirit and their fighting power were blunted. Another captain would have given up the dream as hopeless. But for de Soto the impossible did not exist. Obstacles were but the stepping stones to his goal. Cíbola and all its treasures could still be won.

Traced on a map, the route of de Soto's expedition resembles a shaky letter M scrawled backwards. Starting from the middle of the Florida peninsula, it runs northwards, then slants down obliquely towards the coast to a point just short of the base-line. That point is Mavilla.[1] From there it veers up sharply to the north-west, only to fall south again along the line of the Mississippi. From Mavilla then in the middle of November 1540, the army resumed its march to the north. The country was rough, the natives hostile, and the weather cold and snowy. The Spaniards decided to winter at a fair-

[1] Mobile.

sized settlement called Chicaza, where they were to spend four cheerless months. The natives had abandoned it at their approach, but de Soto thought it prudent to court their friendship, which he did by inviting the chiefs and leading men to dine with him, 'giving them pork to eat, which they so relished, although not used to it, that every night Indians would come to some houses where the hogs slept, a cross-bow shot away from the camp, to kill and carry off what they could of them'. The General was not the sort of man to allow his hospitality to be abused. He ordered guards to intercept the marauders; three were seized, two of whom 'the Governor commanded to be slain, and the survivor had his hands cut off and was sent back to the chief'.

The Indians bided their time to strike back. In March hostile braves gathered in the forest by night and launched an attack which caught the Spaniards off their guard. Taking advantage of a fresh northerly wind the Indians hurled firebrands amongst the thatched huts which soon kindled to a fierce blaze. The General, snatching up a lance and dagger and donning a jacket of quilted cotton, was the first to mount and sally out against them. Others were slower to follow his lead, and in the confusion and swift uproar of the night attack, some fifty horses were burnt to death before their owners could release them. But the beasts which survived, though for the most part riderless, proved the salvation of the Spaniards. Mad with terror, they broke their tethers and rushed wildly through the camp. The thunder of their hooves spread panic in turn amongst the Indians. They fled from the burning huts and made for the shelter of the forest, leaving the Spaniards time to recover from their surprise and organize defence. But losses had been heavy; eleven[1] Spaniards were killed and many wounded, amongst them the General, who had fallen from his horse as there had been no time to tighten the saddle-girth. What few possessions the Spaniards had salvaged from Mavilla

[1] Garcilaso says forty.

now perished in the flames of Chicaza. These included the whole cherished herd of swine, except for a hundred or so of the sucklings who were able to slip through the fence and thus escaped the fate of their elders. The latter were 'so fat with the great amount of food they had found in that place that the lard from them ran for a distance of more than two hundred feet'. Amongst the army's casualties was Francisca de Hinestrosa, one of the very few Spanish women accompanying the expedition. She ran from her hut at the first alarm but, remembering she had left her pearls inside, turned back to fetch them and was trapped in the flames.

The expedition was now in a worse plight even than after Mavilla. Had the Indians returned in force to renew their attacks, it might have been annihilated. The Spaniards suffered cruelly from the cold, for some had been caught practically naked by the night attack, and even the better clad went in tatters like gypsies. Some sought to ward off the cold by huddling round large fires, others by plaiting mats of dried grass to serve as blankets or even garments. De Soto thought with impotent rage of the woollen garments and the belts of gold to be found in distant Cíbola.

By the end of March, the expedition had recovered sufficiently to resume the march – westwards now. Their next encounter was with a stockaded fort manned by a horde of Indians 'with their bodies, legs and arms painted and ochred in red, white, yellow and vermilion in stripes, so that they appeared to be wearing hose and doublets. Some wore feathers, others had horns on their heads, and their faces were blackened and their eyes rouged with vermilion to heighten the ferocity of their aspect.' The place was called Alibamo and seems to have been somewhere in the centre or north of the present State of Mississippi, though its name has shifted to denote the river and neighbouring State of today. The Spaniards carried this stronghold by assault, routed the defenders, and pushed on until they reached the banks of a mighty river. So broad and majestic was it that 'if a man were standing on the far side, it could not be discerned whether he were a man or no'. De Soto had reached the Mississippi.

The army marched along the eastern shore of the great river in search of a place where a crossing might be made, for the banks were precipitous and thickly wooded. At last they reached a clearing which sloped gently to the water's edge. Here they camped for three weeks whilst barges were built. The Indians who paddled over from the far shore to gaze at the newcomers brought gifts and seemed inquisitive rather than hostile. But the Spaniards were taking no chances and frightened them off with crossbow fire. 'They were fine looking men, very large and well built; what with the awnings, the plumes, and the shields, and the pennons, and the number of persons in their fleet, it seemed like a famous armada of galleys.' When the barges were completed, the Spaniards embarked and crossed the Mississippi without serious opposition.

The army then marched up the west bank of the Mississippi towards a district called Pacaha, 'where the Indians said there was gold'. But first the trail led through the territory of a chief called Casqui,[1] whose people were the hereditary enemies of the men of Pacaha. Casqui proved only too ready to accompany the Spaniards against Pacaha and take advantage of this heaven-sent chance to pay off old scores against a tribe which had generally got the better of his own people in war. Besides, they looked upon the Governor as a miracle-worker, and brought out their blind to be healed by him. De Soto had neither the faith nor the desire to work miracles. He contented himself with instructing the interpreters to explain as best they could that there was One in the heavens who had power to make the

[1] In most Spanish accounts, the chiefs and the territory over which they rule bear the same name. Thus the terms Pacaha, Casqui, etc, can denote either the locality or the ruler.

sick whole; that He was the Creator of Earth and Heaven, and had suffered on a Cross for their redemption. Whilst the Indians were puzzling over these words, de Soto had a large wooden cross made and erected in the highest part of the settlement. Before this the Spaniards fell on their knees, exhorting the Indians to do likewise.

The alliance thus sealed by the adoration of the Cross and the hope of rich booty at the expense of a common foe, the Spaniards and their new allies prepared to march against Pacaha. This proved to be a large settlement, surrounded on three sides by a moat filled with water diverted from the Mississippi, which served both for defence and as a means of food supply, for it abounded in fish. The chief of Pacaha did not await the coming of his enemies. He slipped away with his warriors by canoe to an island in the Great River, while the Spaniards and their allies sacked the place at their leisure. The Spaniards rejoiced particularly to find 'many mantles, deer-skins, lion- and bear-skins, and many cat-skins. Many men who had been ill-clad clothed themselves there. Of the mantles they made cloaks and cassocks. Of the deer-skins were made jerkins, shirts, stockings and shoes. And from the bear-skins they made very good cloaks, such as no water could get through. And there they found shields of raw cow-hide out of which they made armour for the horses.'

While the Spaniards were thus re-equipping themselves with the spoils of Pacaha, the chief Casqui sent word that his war-canoes should be brought up the Great River so that the enemy could be pursued to their island lair. The Indians were jubilant to find what advantages alliance with the invincible white men could bring, but their intoxication with booty and revenge nearly proved their undoing. A combined force of Indians and Spaniards now embarked to attack Pacaha's island. More captives, clothing and other valuables fell into their hands, and the Indians promptly loaded the lion's share into their canoes and sailed off downstream with it. This was not at all de Soto's idea of how Indian auxiliaries ought to behave. Besides, what he had seen of the wealth and numbers of Pacaha's subjects began to convince him that, once they had been frightened into submission, they might prove more useful allies than their Casqui rivals. So the Spaniards changed their tactics. Emissaries were sent to Pacaha offering peace and friendship. The chief replied with gifts and assurances of loyalty, and finally presented himself in person before the General. To seal this new alliance, a quick but effective raid was made into Casqui's territory.

Casqui was now thoroughly alarmed, and memory of the indignities he had so lately inflicted on Pacaha made him fear the direst retribution. De Soto summoned the erring and timorous Casqui, who sought to appease the white man's anger by the gift of a nubile daughter and a large quantity of fish and hides. Pacaha, determined to go one better, presented two women – either wives or sisters, for accounts vary – called Macanoche and Mochile. 'They were shapely, tall and ample,' the Gentleman of Elvas relates. 'Macanoche was comely; courtly in her manners and features.' But Mochile he describes merely as 'robust'. These women had in fact already fallen captive to the Spaniards and their Indian master probably suspected that they had been defiled.

De Soto now undertook the unfamiliar role of peacemaker, bidding the rival chiefs dine at his table and be reconciled. But not even his stern pressure could make them forget their feud. The two chiefs were soon disputing the favour of being seated on the Spaniard's right. De Soto quietened them by declaring, somewhat smugly, that 'amongst Christians, one seat is deemed as good as another'. No doubt he considered it to the Spaniards' advantage that the Indians should now cease from inter-tribal warfare, since rumours had just reached him that there was gold to be found in the hills not far off. No time was lost in sending a party to investigate, but the men returned some days later, weak through subsisting on a diet of persimmons and maize stalks, with only a few lumps of metal which turned out to be copper. The land to which they had penetrated[1] held no promise of other riches.

De Soto questioned the natives closely for other clues as to where precious metals and populous cities were to be found. To the south, they now told him, anxious to be rid of such dangerous guests. So to the south the march continued, with many a twist and turn in pursuit of each will-o'-the-wisp, until they reached a region known as Tulla, whose inhabitants they found to be more warlike than any they had yet encountered. The General announced his coming by sending six captured natives with their right hands and their noses cut off to bid the chief do him obedience. The Indians made ready for battle. They set upon the Spaniards not only with bows and arrows, but with long poles the tips of which had been hardened in fire and which they wielded in the manner of pikes. Even when overpowered, these fierce savages would not acknowledge defeat. 'When our Castillians attempted to take them by force,' the Inca Garcilaso reports, 'they simply fell to the ground without uttering a word, giving their captors to understand that their greatest desire was that they should either be slain or left alone.' The women were as fierce-spirited as the men, and stubbornly refused to serve the Spaniards. One who fell to them as a slave was 'of so malevolent a disposition and so ill-tempered and arrogant that if her master or any of his comrades told her what she had to do in regard to cooking or any other of her duties, she would strike them in the face with a pot or a brand from the fire, or whatever else she could lay hands on'. No wonder that when she finally managed to escape, 'her master was glad to find himself delivered of such a shrew'.

The Spaniards remained in the land of Tulla for a few

[1] Probably in the north-east part of the State of Mississippi.

weeks, 'more because of the necessity of treating their
wounded than for any pleasure to be had from stopping in
the land of such evil folk', and then set out in quest of more
favoured parts where they could winter. Ten days' march
away from Tulla was a country called Autiamque which
seemed to offer just what they needed. It was a land of corn-
fields and rich pastures, the Indians told them, and it stood
by the shores of a 'great water'. Could this be an arm of the
sea, de Soto wondered? Surely, after those hundreds of
leagues' wandering, the expedition must be within reach of
the South Sea?[1] They would winter then in Autiamque and
build a couple of brigantines. When spring came, he would
send one to Mexico and the other to Cuba, where his friends
must now have given him up for lost. Two hundred and
fifty of his force had indeed perished. Fresh supplies and
recruits were desperately needed. For Cíbola had yet to be
found and its treasures gained.

Autiamque proved a good place in which to pass the
winter. There were lakes and swamps in abundance, even
though there was no trace of any arm of the sea, and the
Spaniards tried to forget their disappointment by taking
what the land had to offer; abundant supplies of maize, beans
and nuts, lush grass for the horses, and good sport hunting
deer and snaring rabbits. The army found snug quarters in
a large village, from which the natives had been driven, and
fortified it with a stout palisade. If the winter evenings were
long, cards could make the time pass quickly. Gaming was
a passion with the Spaniards – was not the expedition itself
one vast gamble? – and though the packs they had brought
with them had been destroyed at Mavilla and Chicaza, the
Spaniards made good the loss by preparing fresh cards out
of parchment and painting them with loving ingenuity. The
chroniclers tell of one Francisco de Guzmán, a rich hidalgo
of Seville, who was so addicted to gaming that he bartered

---

[1] In reality, the Spaniards were somewhere in south-central Arkansas,
more than a thousand miles from the shores of the Pacific.

away all he had – his clothes, his weapons, his horse – until he was left with a single slave-girl as his only possession. Rather than make this final sacrifice, Guzmán decided to desert and turn native. The girl's father, a native chieftain, gave him asylum, and neither the threats nor the persuasions of the General could induce him to return to the army.

All things considered, the winter at Autiamque was the most tolerable which the Spaniards had spent since they had landed in Florida. But one loss was suffered which proved irreparable. Juan Ortiz, their invaluable and much-tried interpreter, died from the exertions of the long march. Though some of the Indians who accompanied the expedition had picked up a smattering of Spanish, Ortiz was the only man who really understood the mentality of the natives and had a mastery of some of their tongues. 'He could find out in four words what it otherwise took a whole day to discover from the Indians,' the Gentleman of Elvas notes, 'and even then, they would often understand just the opposite of what was asked of them.' Ortiz seems, too, to have been as humane as he was resourceful. Once, when de Soto threatened to execute a couple of Spaniards for disobeying his orders and molesting some Indians with whom the Governor wished to make an alliance, Ortiz managed to twist the words of the envoys whom their chief had sent to complain and persuaded de Soto that the Indians were assuring the General that no harm had been done and that the chief begged the accused would be set free. Juan Ortiz would indeed be missed, by his comrades and by the natives alike.

By March, when the worst of the winter was over, the General gave orders to break camp. He was in a fever of impatience to be on the march again. But which way should he take? On to Cíbola, or back home by the likeliest route? The lure of gold now glinted but feebly through the forest. The Spaniards were adrift in the immensity of the wilderness as in an ocean. The hope of success had all but vanished;

there remained only the hope of survival. And that, it was becoming increasingly clear, could only be realized if the Spaniards could make their way back to the Great River and build barges to carry them down to the sea. So de Soto turned back from the west and marched back in a great south-easterly sweep towards the Mississippi.

In approaching the Great River, the Spaniards passed through the territories of two warring tribes whose chiefs the General was able to play off against each other as he had done with Casqui and Pacaha. He set up his headquarters at Guachoya, the chief settlement of one of them, and sent an expedition against Nilco, the rival stronghold. It was an affair of wanton cruelty – clearly the act of men brutalized and now driven to desperation by their three years' wanderings in the wilderness – for which even contemporary chroniclers can find little justification. The Gentleman of Elvas tells us that the Spaniards and their Guachoya allies fell upon the unsuspecting settlement, 'and when the Captain ordered that the life of no male should be spared, they were so much taken by surprise that not a man amongst them was ready to draw a bow. The cries of the women and children were such as to deafen those who pursued them. About one hundred were slain. Others were allowed to get away sorely wounded, that they might strike terror into those who were absent. Some soldiers were so cruel and butcher-like that they killed all before them, young and old, though little or no resistance was offered.'

After this demonstration, designed to overawe friend and foe alike, the Spaniards returned to their base at Guachoya and began preparations for building the boats. The General, worn out with the fatigues and frustrations of the endless trek, was now beginning to show signs of physical and mental collapse. The nature of his illness is unknown. It may have been malaria, or one of a dozen diseases of which the wilderness was so prolific. Some contemporaries ascribed it rather to mortification, bitterness of spirit, and superstitious despair. An astrologer had once predicted that de Soto would live no longer than his brother-in-law, Vasco Nuñez de Balboa, the discoverer of the South Sea, who had been beheaded at the age of forty-two. De Soto had now reached that age. Garcilaso, who makes no mention of this story in describing the death of his hero, simply says that 'he died of a fever', and we may perhaps leave it at that.

But the urge to discover and to dominate still tormented de Soto, although he no longer had the strength to lead his men in person. On the far side of the Great River, opposite the territory of Guachoya, stretched the lands of a powerful chief whom the Indians called Quigaltam. A raiding party under Juan de Añasco returned with the report that the country was sparsely populated and almost impassable because of the marshes and the canebrakes which flanked the river. The General sent an imperious message from his sick bed to Quigaltam announcing that he was a Child of the Sun to whom tribute was due, and that the chief should come at once to do him obedience. The answer which the Indian returned is a classic of dignified defiance; 'As to what you claim about being a Child of the Sun, I will believe you if you cause him to dry up the Great River. As to the rest, it is not my custom to visit any one; but rather all of whom I ever heard have come to visit me, to serve and obey me, and to pay me tribute, either of their own free will or by force. If you desire to see me, come where I am. If for peace, I will receive you with special favour; if for war, I will await you in my town. But neither for you nor for any man will I set back one foot.'[1]

The defiance of Quigaltam and the realization that he himself was now powerless to teach the Indian a lesson heightened the General's fever; and he saw death approach – a death in the heart of a hostile country, rendered more bitter by the knowledge that he had squandered his fortune

[1] Elvas narrative. Hodge & Lewis, op. cit., p. 229.

and his life, and those of the men under his command, in vain attempts to discover the secret treasures which must now fall to another. He was still feared and obeyed by his men, but resentment burned within them, and 'they neither gave him their companionship, nor visited him, as otherwise they would have done'. According to one account, de Soto had at last resolved, at this late hour, that he would found a settlement on the shores of the Mississippi and try to colonize the land with fresh men and supplies from Cuba and New Spain. This dream was not altogether fantastic; it might have proved possible to open up the vast interior of the continent in this way, just as the lands of the River Plate were being opened up for settlement from Asunción nearly one thousand miles up that river. But now it was too late. The expedition was too worn and depleted for serious settlement, and the General had reached his last hour.

When the time came for de Soto to take formal leave of his officers and chief men, he had them swear obedience to Luís Moscoso de Alvarado, who was proclaimed his successor. On 21 May, 1542, de Soto died, after 'beseeching mercy of the most Holy Trinity, invoking in his favour and protection the blood of Jesus Christ our Lord, and calling for the intercession of the Virgin'.

After de Soto's death, the Spaniards held a Council of War. They resolved to make one more attempt to reach Mexico by marching overland to the west; for they feared the voyage down the Great River and across the sea, and still clung to the shreds of their hope that 'by going overland it might be they would yet discover some rich country that could avail them'. It was an unwise decision; the goal proved as uncertain and distant as ever, the natives as hostile and the country as inhospitable. Moscoso marched on until October, when he turned back once more to the Mississippi which he reached near the spot where de Soto died. There, with great labour, the Spaniards constructed seven brigantines and with these the three hundred survivors of the

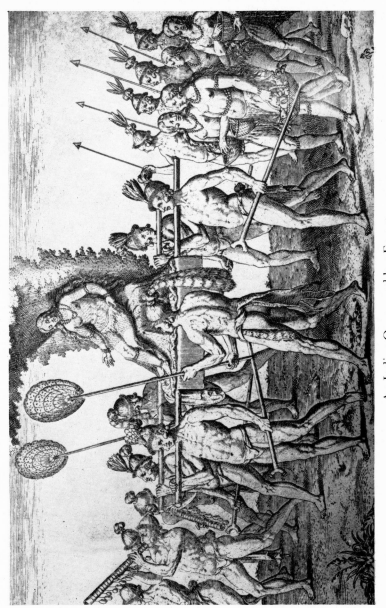

An Indian Queen and her Escort.

Hernan de Soto with vignettes representing the attack on
Alibamo, the battle of Mavilla, and the withdrawal of the
remnants of the expedition from Florida.

expedition, after many further perils and adventures, at length reached the safety of Mexico.

But before Moscoso and his comrades could set out on their last bid to cross the continent on foot, they had first to give their late leader a worthy burial. It was important to conceal from the Indians what had happened, as the death of one who had claimed the respect and obedience due to a demi-god might give the signal for revolt. The body was buried secretly at night, and Moscoso gave out that the General, being a Child of the Sun, had simply ascended into the skies. The chief replied by presenting the Spaniards with two well-grown young men who, if they could not emulate the flight of the demi-god, could at least be slaughtered according to tribal custom and their spirits be released to serve him in the next world. Moscoso, embarrassed by such a pagan offering, replied that the General was only on a celestial visit and that he had taken one soldier with him which would suffice for his needs. But lest the Indians should discover the truth and inflict some indignity on the body of the late general, the Spaniards decided to dig up the corpse and re-bury it in the depths of the Mississippi. So, under cover of darkness, de Soto was given his second burial, wrapped – according to one account – in a shroud weighted down with sand, or – according to another – in the hollowed trunk of a great oak tree.

De Soto is said to have left a will, scribbled in cypher on a scrap of parchment or paper which was all his writing material, but this has never been found. Apart from his possessions in Cuba, he had little to bequeath, and such as there were Moscoso disposed of by public auction amongst his comrades, the cost to be paid – for the ghost of the vision still haunted them – 'at the first melting of gold and silver, or the division of vassals and territory'. His personal possessions were found to consist of two male and three female slaves, three horses, and seven hundred swine. Such was the estate of the man on whom providence had once bestowed the gold of Atahualpa's ransom, and who had staked this fortune on a bid to find one greater still in the mirage cities of the American wilderness.

CHAPTER IX

Coronado conquers the Seven Cities

De Soto's slow agony in the wilderness had left the Viceroy free to prepare a major expedition of his own for the conquest of the Seven Cities. The tales which Friar Marcos had brought back from Cíbola created an immediate and tremendous impression in Mexico. He was received at once by Mendoza who listened eagerly to every detail of his report. Zumárraga, the Bishop of Mexico, was equally enthusiastic. Only Cortés received the news sourly and denounced the Friar as an untrustworthy visionary who had trespassed in regions which Cortés alone had the right to explore, and who passed off other men's discoveries as his own.

The Viceroy's first impulse was to lead the expedition himself, so convinced did he feel of its spectacular success. But affairs of state detained him in the capital, and Mendoza decided to entrust the command to his youthful and energetic protégé, Francisco Vasquez de Coronado, whose military and administrative gifts had raised him to the governorship of New Galicia in place of the discredited Guzmán. While Coronado[1] was collecting his force together, the Viceroy considered that it would be as well – for he was a prudent man, even in his most sanguine projects – to seek independent confirmation of Marcos' reports. For this purpose he commissioned the experienced and clear-headed Captain Melchior Díaz, who had befriended Cabeza

[1] The shortened form of the name is more properly Francisco Vasquez, but he is generally, if less correctly, referred to as Coronado.

de Vaca on the latter's return from his odyssey, to go over the trail followed by the Friar and check the accuracy of his reports. Mendoza also ordered another resourceful officer, Hernando de Alarcón, to prepare a small fleet, coast up the Sea of Cortés, and ascend the unexplored river at its head, with the object of supplying and keeping in touch with Coronado's land-force and, if possible, of reaching the Seven Cities by that route.

The army was at length mustered at Compostela, and while it was moving up to Culiacán, Captain Díaz returned from his reconnaissance. The report which he sent to the Viceroy was kept secret, but enough leaked out to cause some concern. Harsh weather conditions had prevented him from reaching Cíbola itself, but he had questioned many Indians who claimed to know it well. They told him that the Seven Cities consisted of three large and four small settlements. It seemed to be true that their inhabitants dwelt in large and well-built houses, and that 'they have turquoises there in plenty, but not so many as the Friar said'. Of gold, however, there was absolutely no trace; 'they could tell me nothing of any metal there, nor did they say that they had it'. This was far from what Coronado's army of adventurers – or indeed their powerful sponsors – had expected. A shock to morale, right at the outset of the expedition, might have serious consequences. So the watchful Friar, 'noticing that some were feeling alarmed, dispelled these clouds, promising that what they would see should be good, and that he would place them in a country where their hands would be filled.'

In Culiacán, where the Spanish settlers gave them a lavish welcome, Coronado rested his men for a couple of weeks and then decided it would be wise to push on ahead with a picked force of some eighty horsemen, twenty-five to thirty foot soldiers, and a contingent of Mexican auxiliaries. The main body of the army, with beasts and baggage train, was to follow later under the command of Tristan de Luna y

Arellano. On 22 April, 1540, Coronado left Culiacán and followed the route which Friar Marcos, and Captain Díaz after him, had taken. The march was not an easy one, at least for youths fresh to the hardships of campaigning, for they found the coastal plain overgrown with thick undergrowth and slashed at intervals by the stony beds of rivers which men and beasts had often to ford at their peril. But the Indians came out to greet the white men as their friends, for the crosses which Coronado and the friars, following the example of Cabeza de Vaca, Marcos and Díaz, sent out to them, they knew to be the symbols of peace. Such food as they had they hospitably brought out to share with the strangers, and for whatever the Indians offered to the Spaniards, Coronado ordered that gifts should be given in exchange, according to the Viceroy's instructions. Any Spaniard caught seizing food or possessions from an Indian was liable to stern penalties. Nor was it permitted to compel the local Indians to act as carriers, and every soldier, even the proud hidalgos, had to carry his own supplies and equipment. The Spanish soldiers were not allowed to lodge in Indian settlements, even if invited to do so; it was better for the discipline of the army to camp outside and avoid the risk of incidents. Thus, while de Soto's men burned and pillaged their way through Florida, ousting natives from their villages, seizing and enslaving all whom they could lay hands on, the Coronado expedition made an orderly though laborious way towards the Seven Cities.

At length they reached the broad valley of which Friar Marcos had reported rumours of gold and populous settlements. Melchior Díaz was again despatched to reconnoitre. Once more he was obliged to return with a disappointing report; there was no gold, no food and no settlement, apart from a few wretched clusters of huts. Here was another shock for the Spaniards. 'The whole company,' Coronado reported in his despatch to the Viceroy,[1] 'felt disturbed at

[1] G. P. Winship; *The Journey of Coronado*, pp. 159-85.

this, that a thing so much praised, and about which the father had said so many things, should be found so very different; and they began to think that all the rest would be of the same sort.' How Friar Marcos attempted to explain this new disappointment away we do not know. He was in the vanguard, but contemporary accounts have henceforth curiously little to say of him. It was left to the General himself to revive the confidence of the men. 'When I marked this,' he goes on, 'I strove to hearten them as best I could, telling them that Your Lordship had always held that this part of our journey would be a thankless task and that we ought to fix all our thoughts on the Seven Cities and the other lands of which we had report – that those should be the goal of our endeavours.'

So, stilling their misgivings as best they could, Coronado and the vanguard pushed on over the rough track towards the large village of Corazones. The trail was far harder than Marcos had led the men to expect. 'We all marched cheerfully along a very bad track,' Coronado goes on to tell the Viceroy, 'where it was impossible to pass without making a fresh road or repairing the one which was there, which troubled the soldiers not a little, considering that everything the Friar had said proved to be quite the reverse. For the father had said and declared, amongst other things, that the road would be plain and good, and that there would be only one small hill for about half a league. But the truth is that there are mountains which, however well the road might be laid, cannot be crossed without grave danger of the horses falling over the side. Indeed, it was so bad that many of the beasts which Your Lordship sent as food for the army were lost on this part of the route because of the roughness of the rocks.'

On 26 May, just over a month after leaving Culiacán, Coronado entered Corazones. The inhabitants were, as ever, friendly, but they had little food to spare since the maize was not yet ripe, and Coronado was obliged to send the indispensable Melchior Dìaz ahead to procure supplies by barter from the more fertile valley of Sonora. Ten or twelve of the horses, and a number of negro slaves and Indian auxiliaries, had already succumbed to the rigours of the march. Men and beasts were in dire need of nourishment, and while the expedition halted at Corazones, messengers were sent to the coast to learn whether anything had been seen of the ships which the Viceroy had ordered to sail along the coast to the head of the great gulf. They returned with a vague story that a ship had been sighted some time ago not far from land, but whether this was a vessel from Ulloa's expedition[1] of the year before, or one of the Viceroy's ships, or even a foreign interloper, was not clear. Coronado was worried lest Alarcón's small fleet, with its precious supplies, had come to grief. He was disturbed too to discover that the trail he was following had already begun to veer away from the sea and headed inland, so that he soon found himself fifteen days' journey away from the coast, 'albeit the father had said it was only five leagues and that he had seen it. We all became very distrustful,' the General added, 'and felt great anxiety and dismay to see that everything was the reverse of what he had told Your Lordship.'

The trail now led up the Sonora valley and then across rugged country leading to the ruins of an ancient settlement known by the natives as Chichilticale, or the Red House. 'It was made of coloured or reddish earth,' Castañeda relates. 'It appeared to have been a strong place at some former time when it was inhabited, and it was very plain that it had been built by a civilized and warlike race of strangers.' Its ruinous state however further damped the spirits of the Spaniards, and even the General 'was much affected on seeing that the fame of Chichilticale was summed up in one tumbledown and roofless house'. Here the Spaniards rested for a couple of days, and would have stayed longer, were

[1] See p. 81.

not their provisions running dangerously low. Beyond them stretched the wild, beautiful, but inhospitable tract of country which seperated them, as they believed, from the Seven Cities. Pausing to slake their thirst at one of the mountain streams, some of Coronado's men were driven by hunger to gather and eat of the wild herbs which grew near by. One Spaniard, two negroes, and a number of Indian auxiliaries died from exhaustion and the poisonous effects of these plants.

Coronado was now within a few days' march of Cíbola, and he resolved to proceed with redoubled caution. It was only too likely that the inhabitants of the Seven Cities would prove hostile. Had they not killed Estebán, the Spaniards' emissary, and would they not now be prepared to defend their cities, and the hoarded wealth, against the invaders they must know would follow? Coronado ordered García Lopez de Cárdenas, the maestre de campo, to push on with a band of picked horsemen. For two days this vanguard rode on, through open, rolling country, until they reached the banks of a small river. Its waters were red with the mud carried down by the spring spate, and they named it Río Vermejo – the Red River. Here they caught their first sight of the Indians of Cíbola. Four men came towards the Spaniards making signs of peace and giving them to understand that they would be welcome. On the next day, the Indians declared, their people would come out with gifts of food. Cárdenas answered by giving them a cross in token of friendship, and bidding them return to their city and tell the people to remain where they were and have no fear, since the Spaniards 'were coming in the name of His Majesty to help and defend them'. Two of the Indians were retained as hostages, and Cárdenas sent a messenger back to report to his General that he had made contact with the men of Cíbola.

On receiving this message, Coronado hurried on to join the vanguard. If the Indians really desired peace, Cíbola might be occupied as easily as the other settlements through which the Spaniards had passed; but was this only a ruse which would allow the Indians to spy out the strength of the strangers and take them off their guard? Coronado presented the two hostages with cloaks and paternosters, and repeated the assurances which Cárdenas had given them. Then he sent his maestre de campo forward again with orders to seize any passes or dangerous passages where the Indians might think to stage an ambush. Late the same night a breathless courier reported to the General that the Indians had attacked the vanguard but had been driven off. Cárdenas had caught sight of Indians observing the approach of the white men from the summit of a hill. He had sent a cross and other gifts to them, and had repeated his protestations of peace. The Indians had gone off, seemingly well pleased, but had returned later the same night in force. Mounted guards had given the alarm in time, though some of the horses were stampeded by the shouting and the shower of arrows falling out of the darkness. But Cárdenas had rallied his men and ridden out against the enemy, although no prisoners could be taken as the natives knew the ground and managed to slip away.

Coronado now realized that Cíbola would not, after all, fall into his hands without a struggle. The sooner the decisive engagements could be fought the better, for provisions were all but exhausted and the men 'were in such great need of food that I thought we should all die of hunger if we continued to lack supplies for another day'. So, spurred by hunger and expectation of combat, the Spaniards pressed forward towards Cíbola. They knew from the plumes of smoke which streaked the sky-line as they advanced that the Indians were forewarned of their coming.

The trail led up a narrow valley. Another group of four or five Indians was encountered, and Cárdenas rode on alone to speak to them, but they turned and made off. Then, looking beyond the fleeing natives, and across a stretch of level, open ground, he could see the walls of an Indian settlement. The Spaniards had reached their goal; the first of the fabled Seven Cities of Cíbola stood before them.

It was a moment of dramatic expectation. Another Mexico, with its barbaric splendours and inexhaustible treasures was about to be revealed. There were assuredly many in Coronado's army who had talked with Cortés' veterans and heard from their own lips descriptions of the unforgettable vision which met their gaze when they first looked down upon the lake and the great city of Tenochtitlán. Bernal del Castillo related that 'when we saw so many cities and villages built in the water and other great towns on dry land, and that straight and level causeway leading to Mexico, we were amazed and said that it was like the enchantments they tell of in the legend of Amadis, on account of the great towers and temples and buildings rising from the water and all built of masonry. And some of our soldiers even asked whether the things we saw were not a dream. . . . Gazing on such marvellous sights, we did not know what to say, or whether what appeared before us was real; for on one side, on the land, there were great cities, and in the lake ever so many more, whilst the lake itself was crowded with canoes, and in the causeway were many bridges built at intervals, and in front of us stood the great city of Mexico itself.'

And Cíbola? Here, too, the Spaniards must have stood speechless at what they saw; speechless, though, not from admiration but from anger and disappointment. Instead of another glittering Aztec city, they saw before them a mean, tenement-like huddle of stone and adobe buildings. The Spaniards, in short, had come upon the dwellings, or pueblos, of the tribes who later became known as Pueblo Indians. Castañeda, the soldier chronicler, has only a terse comment of contempt: 'It is a little, cramped village, looking as if it had been all crumpled up together. . . . When they saw it, such were the curses that some hurled at Friar Marcos that I pray God may protect him from them.'

But the shock of disillusionment was speedily followed by a call to action. On the level ground in front of the settlement, some three hundred Indian braves were drawn up in two detachments to await the invaders. They carried bows and arrows, leather shields, and wooden war-clubs, and with defiant gestures they bade the Spaniards turn back and not dare to cross the symbolic border lines which they had marked off on the ground with sacred corn-meal. For the last time, Cárdenas rode forward, escorted by a handful of horsemen, two friars (but not Marcos, who must have had good reasons of his own now for keeping to the rear) and a notary. The latter then delivered a harangue, in accordance with the Crown's standing instructions that Indians must first be exhorted to submit peacefully, summoning them to accept the new faith and the sovereignty of the Emperor, briefly and no doubt bewilderingly presented to them with the aid of an interpreter. But the men of Cíbola were in no mood to respond to the exhortation, even if they could make anything of it. 'Being a proud people,' Coronado records, they paid but little heed, 'because it seemed to them we were few in number and they would have little or no difficulty in overcoming us.' A flight of arrows greeted the notary's harangue, penetrating his armour and wounding his horse. Another arrow pierced the gown of one of the friars, but 'blessed be God, did him no harm'.

The General attempted a final gesture of conciliation in person. Urging his men to remain calm in face of this provocation, he rode forward to the Indians holding out a number of gifts. But the Spaniards' forbearance only emboldened the Indians, so that they 'came up almost to the heels of our horses to discharge their arrows'. The situation was now dangerous, for the Indians heavily outnumbered the Spaniards, who were exhausted by the long march and weakened by lack of food. Peaceful persuasion had failed.

It was now the hour to strike. Invoking St James, the patron saint of Spain, with their war-cry of 'Santiago!', Coronado's men charged. The Indians were speedily scattered. Some fled over the plain where the horsemen would have run them down if the General had not called them back, but most of them retreated hastily behind the walls of their town. Ten or twelve lost their lives.

Coronado lost no time in following up this success and ordered a general assault. Behind the adobe walls, he knew, was stored the food which, for the moment, the Spaniards coveted more than all the gold and jewels they had come to find. Hunger drove them to the assault, as it drove, through the centuries, the nomadic Indians of the plains to raid the sedentary tribes who cultivated their fields and garnered their crops.

The town which the Spaniards were now attacking was unlike anything they had yet seen in the New World. It was built of stone and adobe, all the houses forming a single compact structure like a vast tenement building of pyramidal shape. The lower part formed a defensive wall, without windows, and with but a single doorway. Above the wall was a terrace, where the warriors crowded with their bows and arrows and made ready to hurl down missiles from the piles of stones they had heaped up for that purpose. Behind this terrace rose another block of houses, behind this again ascending tiers of buildings, so that the summit of the urban pyramid was composed of houses four or five storeys in height. Access to the terraces was by steps cut in walls, or by ladders which the natives could remove at will. The whole settlement was composed of some two hundred individual rooms or houses, and might ordinarily contain a population of up to one thousand. At the news of the Spaniards' coming, women and children had been sent off to safety elsewhere, and their place taken by warriors from neighbouring towns.

Coronado deployed his forces so as to surround the place

and ordered his horsemen to dismount while the musketeers and crossbowmen attempted to drive the Indians from their commanding positions on the terraces. The fire of these exhausted troops had little effect, for 'the crossbowmen broke all the strings of their bows and the musketeers could do nothing, because they had arrived so weak and feeble they could scarcely stand on their feet'. Coronado, a magnificent figure in crested helmet and gilded armour, led the storming party in person. The defenders continued to hurl down stones and arrows from their vantage point, singling out the General for special attack. Twice he was felled by heavy stones and was only saved from death by the stoutness of his helmet. As he lay on the ground half stunned, Cárdenas and another cavalier, Hernando de Alvarado, gallantly threw themselves over his body to protect him from further missiles. Then, as the assault continued, he was carried from the battle more dead than alive, with two face wounds, his leg pierced by an arrow, and his body covered with bruises. When he returned to consciousness, it was to learn that his men, fired by his valiant example, had carried the day and that the first of the Seven Cities, Háwikuh,[1] with ample stores of food, was in their hands. 'After this,' Castañeda tersely concludes, 'the whole country was at peace.'

In the days which followed, while the General recovered from his wounds and his men ate their fill of the maize, beans, dried squashes and other food found in the storehouses which composed almost the whole of the ground floor of the terraced village, Coronado was able to take stock of the strange land to which the Spaniards come. The adventurers had seen from the first glance that this was far from being the city of their dreams. Yet the place gave signs of a civilization of an unusual kind. Its inhabitants, though not comparable in numbers, wealth or sophistication

[1] See p. 143.

with the subjects of the Aztec or the Inca empires, led an ordered life, with peculiar and highly developed social institutions.

The origins of these Indians, whom their neighbours sometimes called the Anasazi or Ancient People, was lost in legend. Their ancestors were the Basket-Maker Indians who, in the first centuries of our era, had begun to exchange the life of hunters for that of cultivators of maize and squash. These people soon developed skill in pottery and in weaving baskets and textiles, and experimented with house building. Influences, and possibly some immigration, from the more highly civilized races from the south certainly speeded the process of growth. From the beginning of the eighth century skills and techniques were adapted to the local environment and developed to form the characteristic pueblo culture; the arts of building in stone and adobe, cultivating corn and irrigating the land, and making beautiful coiled pottery and soft robes fashioned from the feathers of turkeys which they bred for this purpose. For some four centuries their simple civilization had bloomed. The people, concentrated and secure in their tenement-like homes, developed a thriving trade and culture. The wealth which came to them was coverted into beads and finely worked ornaments of turquoise, sea-shells, and coloured stone, for they did not know the use of metals. A beautiful and complex ritual of ceremonies designed to propitiate the water-gods was evolved, and the life of the communities developed in patterns of increasing social complexity.

Some two hundred and fifty years before the Spaniards came, a decline had set in. We do not know its exact causes, but the attacks of the nomadic tribes and dissensions amongst the different pueblos must have played their part. Recurrent cycles of drought had also occurred, searing the corn-fields and forcing the people to seek new homes where the rain-gods would look on them with greater favour. The ruins of Chichilticale, which the Spaniards had seen on their march, were evidence that the power and extent of the pueblo civilization had once been far greater.

The pueblo in which the Spaniards were now quartered was in all probability Háwikuh, the most westerly of the group of settlements which were strung out for a distance of some fifteen miles along the valley of the Zuñi River which rises in the mountains of the same name and flows from New Mexico into Arizona, where it joins the Little Colorado, or the Río Vermejo as the Spaniards first called it. The whole of this tribal range was known by the Indians as Shiwina – the name which Friar Marcos recorded as Cíbola, or Cívola, as some chroniclers wrote it. All but one of the 'Seven Cities' have now been identified. Beside Háwikuh, there was Mátsaki, described by the Spaniards as the largest of the group, Hálona, whose site is near the modern village of Zuñi where the two thousand surviving descendents of the Indians of Cíbola live today, Kiákima, on the flanks of the Thunder Mountain and overlooking the scorched red Zuñi plain, and two other pueblos called Kechipáuan and Kwákina. Today the magic has faded from the name of Cíbola, no less alluring and fabulous in its time than El Dorado, but it has not been altogether lost from memory. Beyond Cíbola lay the great plains with their vast herds of bison, which the Spaniards often referred to as 'vacas de Cíbola', and *cíbolo* is still the Spanish word for bison.

How much, or how little, of the general picture was understood at the moment of the Spanish impact can be gathered from the dispatch which Coronado wrote to the Viceroy four weeks after taking Háwikuh.[1] First of all, the General wished to make it clear that everyone, from His Lordship down to the neediest adventurer, had been thoroughly misled by the Friar Marcos: 'I can assure you that in reality he has not told the truth in a single thing he relates, but everything is just the opposite of what he said,

[1] Winship, op. cit.

except the name of the city and the large stone houses. For although they are not adorned with turquoises nor made of mortar or good bricks, they are very good houses all the same, with three, four, and five storeys, where there are very good apartments and good rooms with corridors; there are also some very good rooms underground and paved, which are made for winter and are something like a sort of hot bath.'

These *kivas*, or subterranean hot-rooms as Coronado describes them, are indeed a marked feature of the pueblos, but their purpose was only imperfectly grasped by the Spaniards. They served as a sort of club-room where the men could gather to do their weaving and tell tribal folk-tales in winter, as Coronado had surmised; but in them the Indians would also hold their mysterious ceremonies, the ritual dances and initiation rites jealously guarded from the eyes of intruders. The *kivas* were built half, or sometimes wholly, underground, in the fashion of the primitive dwellings of the Indians' ancestors, and they were entered by means of a ladder leading down from an opening in the roof, like the hatch of a ship. The walls were often decorated with symbolic paintings whilst designs of religious significance, ingeniously patterned out of coloured sands, were laid out on the floor. At one end of the *kiva* stood a stone or piece of wood with a round hole in it, emblem of the tribe's place of origin and means of communicating with the spirit world. Behind this orifice rose a sort of altar, whilst all round the room ran a stone-capped seat, giving the chamber something of the aspect of a chapter-house.

Of the actual ceremonies practised in the *kivas* and the general religious beliefs which pervaded the whole life of the Pueblo Indians, Coronado has little to say beyond observing – with fair accuracy – that 'so far as I can find out, water is what these Indians worship, because they say it makes the corn grow and sustains their life'. The elaborate and dramatic ritual through which the Indians enacted their

Indians attacking a settlement with burning arrows.

Florida and the North Coast of the Gulf of Mexico. A chart believed to have been drawn by survivors of the de Soto expedition, circa 1543.

myths and invoked the favours of the spirit world – a ritual in which dancing, music, and the wearing of symbolic masks and costumes was imaginatively combined – lay so far outside the experience and comprehension of the Spaniards that only the most garbled accounts were recorded by the early chroniclers. Melchior Díaz, in his journey of reconnaissance, had gathered something by hearsay and devoted the following uncomprehending remarks to it in his report: 'The Indians have their dances and songs, with some flutes which have holes on which to place the fingers. They make much noise. They sing in unison with those who play, and those who sing clap their hands in our fashion. One of the Indians that accompanied Estebán the negro, who had been a captive here, saw the playing as they practised it, and others singing as I have said, although not very vigorously. They say that five or six play together, and that some of the flutes are better than others.' How, behind such antics and discordant noises, could pious Catholics apprehend the poetic invocation of the Indian Rain-Beings, or suspect that these pagans too had their noble myth of the Creation, through the union of Mother Earth and Father Sky?

The inhabitants of Cíbola, Coronado went on to report to the Viceroy, seemed to be of normal size and intelligence, but it puzzled him that natives who went naked except for the breech-clouts they wore beneath a mantle of cotton, hide or rabbit-skin, could yet have the skill to construct such large and well-built dwellings. The intricate and close-knit social structure of these pueblo communities, in which every member was accorded his clearly defined duties and privileges from the moment his parents performed the picturesque ceremony of 'presenting the child to the Sun', were likewise outside the Spaniards' experience. The pattern of chieftain and vassal, familiar to the Spaniards in varying forms from Florida to Peru, was lacking here. 'As far as I could discover or observe,' Coronado wrote to the Viceroy, describing how he had bid the Indians send their lord to him, 'none of these towns have any, since I have not seen any powerful house by which any superiority over others could be shown.' Nor could the Spaniards easily get sight of the Indians' womenfolk, for they had all been sent away, with the children, to places of safety from which they refused to emerge. Here there was no light-hearted giving of women to the Spaniards; such presumptions may indeed have contributed towards the fate of Estebán. Coronado notes the respect and affection which the Zuñis had for their womenfolk, and remarks that 'they love them more than their own selves'. Amongst the Pueblo Indians, the status of women has indeed always been exceptionally high. Monogamy was the rule, and though divorce was not difficult, the wife could exercise the same right as her husband in getting rid of an unsatisfactory partner. It was the women too who were the property-owners. Though the men might build it, the room or 'house', together with its furnishings, belonged to the woman and her rule in this domain was as absolute as that of any lady of Castille. The women were skilled in the making of lovely pottery and were excellent cooks. 'They make the best corn-cakes I have ever seen anywhere,' Coronado noted, 'and this is what everyone normally eats' – a detail of no small account to men who had made the long march from Mexico on short rations.

Of riches other than a copious store of food and some supplies of clothing, the Seven Cities seemed lamentably innocent. Two fragments of emerald and 'some little broken stones which approach the colour of rather poor garnets', and a few stone crystals were the sum of all the booty taken, and even this paltry haul was subsequently mislaid through the carelessness of one of Coronado's servants. Even turquoises were hard to come by, since most had been removed and hidden, though we know that the Zuñis had these gems in plenty, and a necklace with more than twenty-five hundred beads in it has lately come to light. As for gold and silver, only one or two very small pieces had been found, and the Spaniards had not yet managed to induce the Indians to tell where they got them from; 'but I trust in God they will not be able to avoid answering much longer'. There were certainly no mines in Cíbola, and the natives did not know how to work metal. Whence then had these few fragments of gold and silver come? From the other kingdoms, perhaps, greater and more splendid than Cíbola, such as Acus of which Friar Marcos had spoken? But the Friar was now thoroughly discredited, and enquiries from the natives revealed that 'the kingdom of Acus is a single small city',[1] Totonteac a mere cluster of houses, and as for the mighty kingdom of Marata, 'it cannot be found, nor do these Indians know anything about it'. 'God knows,' the disconsolate General concluded, 'that I wish I had better news to write to Your Majesty. But I must give you the truth.' Though Cíbola had proved the bitterest of disappointments, and the other visions of Friar Marcos the merest fantasies, Coronado was resolved that his Spaniards, who had come so far to win their prize, should march on to other lands until they found it.

---

[1] The celebrated pueblo of Acoma, built on the top of a steep cliff. See p. 152.

CHAPTER X

On to Quivira

The force which had captured Cíbola was only the vanguard of the main expedition which had been left to advance by slow stages from Culiacán. Events had moved so quickly under Coronado's leadership that the rest of the army had only reached the Sonora valley when, in the middle of September, it was met by a detachment sent back by the General from Cíbola with news of what had occurred there and with fresh instructions for the march. While Juan Gallego, one of Coronado's most resourceful and audacious captains, rode on post-haste with despatches for the Viceroy, Melchior Díaz came with instructions to establish a garrison in Sonora, where supplies could be easily assured, and then to reconnoitre the country to the west with a view to finding the great river up which, it was hoped, Alarcón was bringing his supply ships. With Gallego and Díaz there also came a crestfallen Friar Marcos, 'because', relates Castañeda, 'he did not deem it safe to stay at Cíbola, seeing that his report had turned out to be entirely false, because the kingdoms he had told about had not been found, nor the populous cities, nor the wealth of gold, nor the precious stones which he had reported, nor the fine clothes, nor other things that had been announced from the pulpits'.

Díaz established his garrison, but committed the mistake of leaving it under the command of Diego de Alcaráz, whose ways with Indians and Spaniards had proved a bitter experience for Cabeza de Vaca. Díaz then pushed on towards the great river, finding the barren regions inhabited by a tribe of Indians, immensely tall, primitive, and poverty-stricken who 'on account of the great cold carry a firebrand (*tisón*) in the hand as they go, with which they warm the other hand and the body as well, and in this way they keep shifting it every now and then'. So the Spaniards christened the river, which we know as the Colorado, the Río del Tisón, or the Firebrand River.

From the natives Díaz learned that a ship, bearing a white chief with a long golden beard and magnificent manners, had sailed up the river not long before. After some searching, the Spaniards found a message nailed to a tree-trunk: 'Alarcón reached this place; letters at the foot of the tree.' Díaz dug and found them, but the contents were a disappointment. Alarcón reported that he had waited in vain at this place for news of the army. He had wished to strike inland himself and reach Cíbola, but hostile tribes and lack of guides forced him to turn back. So he had sailed down the Firebrand River again to report to the Viceroy. His going was a loss to the expedition. Alarcón was an engaging and eccentric figure, of a stamp seldom found in the ranks of the conquistadores. He was a humorist who entered with enormous gusto into his role as Child of the Sun, and who possessed a knack of getting on well with the natives. He engaged them in badinage and soon had them vying with each other for the honour of towing his ship up the river. One regrets that his gifts were not allowed free play in a wider field of operations.

Díaz crossed the Firebrand River on rafts and was exploring beyond when he suffered a fatal hunting accident. His men turned back, bearing their captain on a litter, but he died within three weeks. With the passing of honest Melchior Díaz, there was no one to check the excesses of Alcaráz, and before many months had passed, he had provoked a rising of the hitherto friendly natives and a mutiny of his own garrison.

The main body of the army, meanwhile, had marched on to Cíbola, where Coronado was actively despatching reconnaissance parties with a view to further exploration and conquest in the west. Reports had been received of another group of 'cities', similar to those of Cíbola and also said to be seven in number, some twenty-five leagues distant. This region, which the natives called Tusayan, is familiar today as the land of the Hopis, famous for their Snake Dance and their beautiful pottery. A small party under Captain Pedro de Tovar and Friar Juan de Padilla, who had himself been a fighting man in his youth, was sent across the desert to demand its submission. The natives were unprepared for the coming of the Spaniards, although they had heard alarming rumours that Cíbola had been captured by 'very fierce people who rode about on beasts which ate people'.

The Spaniards camped under one of the high mesas or rocky plateaux on which the Hopis chose to build their towns. In the morning, the inhabitants sallied out ready to do battle should the strangers cross the lines of corn-meal which they drew on the ground, as the men of Cíbola had done. Pedro de Tovar replied by causing the interpreters to declare the formal summons to submission. The Indians showed no signs of yielding, a few blows were exchanged, and the fighting friar urged his captain 'to give the Santiago'. Before the sudden onslaught of the Spaniards the Indians scattered in panic, and soon sued for peace. Gifts were exchanged in token of friendship, and delegations received from the other Hopi pueblos with like protestations of obedience.

When Tovar returned to report to Coronado, he brought news of a large river which the Indians said was not far beyond Tusayan. The General listened with interest. Might this be the same as the river flowing into the great gulf up which Alarcón had been ordered to sail with his supply ships, and which Melchior Díaz had reached from Sonora valley? A fresh party, under Cárdenas, who had led the vanguard to Cíbola, was sent out to explore. Cárdenas rode to Tusayan, where he was well received and given guides, and then on for another twenty days until the way was barred by a stupendous gorge, 'which' – says Castañeda – 'seemed to be more than three or four leagues as the crow flies across to the other side'. The Spaniards had reached the Grand Canyon. For three days they rode along its precipitous edge in search of a way down. Seen from this height, the river looked 'as if it were six feet across, though the Indians said it was half a league wide. . . .' Two adventurous spirits tried to climb down the gorge but were forced to turn back after making only a third of the descent. Up on the plateau not a drop of water was to be found, and since they were unable to reach the river at the bottom of the abyss, the Spaniards were reluctantly obliged to turn back to Cíbola. The line of the Grand Canyon marks the limit of their furthest thrust westwards.

While these parties were probing Tusayan and beyond, Coronado received an embassy which was to deflect the main course of the expedition towards the east. Two chiefs appeared at his headquarters, one of them an old man, the other a tall, well set-up moustachioed young fellow whom the Spaniards nicknamed Bigotes or Whiskers. These men said they had come from a town which they called Cicuye, better known in subsequent history as Pecos, seventy leagues to the east of Cíbola. Bigotes and his fellow chieftain declared that they wished to be friends with the Spaniards and offered to lead them to their country. Gifts were exchanged; from the Indians 'tanned hides and shields and head-pieces, whilst the general gave them some glass dishes and a number of pearls and little bells which they prized highly, as these were things they had never seen'. They spoke of the land they came from, which the Spaniards gathered lay in the valley of a river on the borders of the pueblo country and of the great plains. They also had much to say of 'some cattle which, from a picture that one of them had painted on his skin, seemed to be cows, though from the hides this did not seem possible, since the hair was woolly and snarled, so that we could not tell what kind of skins they had'. This new land seemed intriguing and certainly worth investigating. So Coronado despatched a force of twenty men to undertake a reconnaissance and to return within eighty days. He placed it under the command of Hernando de Alvarado, one of the captains who had saved Coronado's life by valiantly throwing himself over the General's prostrate body at the storming of Cíbola, and who was now to play an important part in the further fortunes of the expedition.

Alvarado started off at the end of August, travelling east past the imposing ruins of once thriving, stone-built pueblos, until they found themselves beneath the mountain stronghold of Ácus or Acoma, 'so high up that it was a very good musket that could throw a ball so far'. Acoma was a lair of robbers, feared far and wide, and it could only be reached by a steep flight of steps which gave place, near the summit, to nothing but a series of holes and ledges which served the agile natives just as well. The top of the cliff, where piles of stones were stored in readiness to repel an invader, was flat and broad enough to enable the Indians to sow crops and store water in natural cisterns. It was strange that the inhabitants now chose to leave this impregnable position and draw up in the valley below, behind their symbolic lines of corn-meal, to bar the Spaniards' way. But when they perceived that the strangers were resolved to pass at all costs, they suddenly changed their tactics, declared themselves for peace, and sealed the pledge by a strange ritual, 'which is to touch the horses and take the sweat and rub themselves with it, and to make crosses with their fingers'. Gifts of turkey, corn, bread, and deerskins were bestowed on the Spaniards, after which the Indians returned to their fortress, where their descendents live today, proud of dwelling in what is probably the oldest continuously inhabited settlement to be found in the United States of America.

Three days later the Spaniards came to a river. It was the Río Grande, and the country around was known as

Tiguex, after its inhabitants, the Tigua Indians. The two chiefs were approaching their home country, and Bigotes went on upstream to give tidings of the strangers' coming. The following day, the chiefs of twelve pueblos paid Alvarado a ceremonious visit, with much playing of flutes and presenting of gifts. It was a fertile country, with fields of maize, beans, and melons. Beyond this group of settlements, Alvarado was told, some seventy or eighty other pueblos were to be found, all similar in type to Cíbola but built of stone in place of adobe. Some of these places he visited as he marched upstream, raising crosses which the friendly natives proceeded to adorn with plumes and roses. They came at last to a very large pueblo which the Indians called Braba, the Taos which artists today know and admire for its picturesque beauty. From this point, Alvarado decided to turn back downstream, sending Coronado samples of the local produce – loads of clothing, tanned skins, 'the head of a cow' – together with a map and a report on the fertility of the land, urging the General to winter his army there rather than in Cíbola.

Alvarado then left the friendly Río Grande valley and headed for new country – the unexplored world of the Great Plains. The obliging Bigotes still guided him, and together they came to his own pueblo of Pecos, where the people gave their chiefs a rousing welcome and bestowed gifts on the Spaniards, including a number of turquoises taken, no doubt, from the mines of Los Cerrillos nearby. Pecos stood at the border between pueblo land, with its cultivated fields and its settled communities, and the boundless land ocean where the nomadic tribes roamed. Here the pueblo-dwellers passed when they ventured out on an occasional buffalo hunt, and here the prairie Indians came to barter their hides and meat.

By the time they reached Pecos, Bigotes announced that he had had enough of travelling and prayed to be excused from accompanying the Spaniards any further. As guides he offered instead two of his personal slaves; one named Sopete, a native of a land called Quivira, the other (whom the Spaniards promptly nicknamed 'The Turk', 'because he looked like one') from the still remoter region known to the Indians as Harahey. In early October, with these two men as guides, Alvarado began the exploration of the Great Plains.

Within a few days the Spaniards gained their first glimpse of the vast herds of roaming buffalo – 'so many, that I know not what to compare them with, unless it be the fish of the sea'. They could be dangerous when attacked; but the Spaniards soon discovered the best ways of dispatching them. They could be felled by a musket shot when stationary, or by spears if attacked on the run. The Indians often preferred to stampede them over the brink of a ravine and destroy the beasts by the score. But strange and exciting as the new sport of buffalo hunting might be, it paled before the accounts which the Indian guides soon began to give of the land which lay ahead. Quivira, declared the Turk, was not only rich in food and cloth, but there were gold and silver to be had there in plenty. When the Spaniards, mindful of Friar Marcos' fantasies, questioned him more closely, the Turk vowed he could give irrefutable proof of what he said. In his own country, he declared, he had once possessed a bracelet of solid gold. This had been seized from him by Bigotes, his master. Let the Spaniards make the chief disgorge it, and they would see he was not lying.

The news of the golden bracelet caused a sensation amongst the Spaniards. The eighty days time limit set by the General was nearly up, and Alvarado decided to hasten back to Pecos and lay his hands on the precious ornament. The chiefs gave him a friendly welcome, but denied all knowledge of any bracelet; the slave, Bigotes declared, must simply be lying. Alvarado stormed and threatened, but when the chiefs continued to profess utter ignorance, he ordered his men to put them in chains. This high-handed action against their respected leaders filled the natives with indignation. They heaped reproaches on the Spaniards as ungrateful and perfidious guests. Was this the way that Christians repaid trust, hospitality, and friendship? They clamoured for the release of their chiefs and loosed off arrows in anger against the Spaniards. Relations between the white men and the Pecos Indians, hitherto so spontaneously friendly, had taken a sudden lamentable turn for the worse.

The events that followed were confused. The Turk, whose words had started all the mischief, vanished. Alvarado suspected that the chiefs had resolved to get rid of an embarrassing witness, and he vowed he would not strike off their chains until the slave was restored. The Turk duly reappeared, but the chiefs were still held prisoner. There followed a short interlude when Spaniards and Pecos Indians made common cause against a neighbouring tribe. Exactly what occurred is not clear, but it seems that the campaign was broken off, and Alvarado decided to report at once to his General, taking along the three main protagonists – Bigotes, the old chief, and the slave – in chains. Coronado, in the meantime, had resolved to follow the advice contained in Alvarado's earlier despatch and to bring up his army to winter in Tiguex. Cárdenas was accordingly sent on to prepare suitable quarters in the Río Grande valley, where he met Alvarado returning with his prisoners. Little could be done to clear up the mystery of the golden bracelet until the General arrived and could draw his own conclusions. In the meantime, the Indians of Tiguex were prevailed upon to vacate one of their twelve pueblos, Alcanfor, for the use of the main Spanish army. The Indians complied, but with very bad grace.

As soon as Coronado reached Tiguex, the Turk was brought before him and proceeded to sing the praises of Quivira with an eloquence which seems to have left a deep impression on the usually clear and prudent mind of the commander. 'The Turk said that in this country there was a river in the level country which was two leagues wide,' Castañeda relates, 'in which there were fishes as big as horses, and large numbers of very big canoes, with more than twenty oarsmen a side, that they carried sails and that their lords sat on the poop under awnings, and on the prow they had a great golden eagle. He also said that the lord of that land took his afternoon siesta under a great tree on which were hung a great number of little golden bells, which lulled him to sleep as they swung in the air. He said too that everyone had their ordinary dishes made of wrought silver, and the jugs and bowls were of gold. He called gold *acochis*. For the time being he was believed, because he related it all so plausibly and because they showed him metal ornaments and he recognized them and said they were not gold, for he knew gold and silver very well and did not care a fig about other metals.'

Could there be any truth in these extraordinary tales of Quivira? The Turk kept vowing that, to prove it, the Spaniards had only to make the chiefs give up the bracelet, while the chiefs as vehemently denied that they had any such thing. One day, apparently with the connivance of Coronado, Alvarado had his two captives taken out to a field and the dogs turned on them. The seizure and bating of the friendly chiefs reads like an episode from de Soto's expedition rather than Coronado's, or a reflection, seen through the distorting mirror of Alvarado's greed-obsessed mind, of Cortés' capture of Montezuma, or Pizarro's capture and execution of Atahualpa. The purpose seems to have been to frighten the chiefs of Tiguex into divulging whatever they might know about the gold, rather than to do them serious injury. Bigotes and the old chief had nothing to say, and the savage dogs were called off. The victims' wounds were bandaged up, but they were not released from custody. They, no less than the talkative Turk, might be needed when the spring came and an expedition could be sent to discover the truth about Quivira.

But first there were other more pressing matters to be settled. The Indians of Tiguex, who had once given Alvarado and his men so warm a welcome, had been provoked to far. To fête a band of strangers for a few days was one thing; to put up a numerous army for a whole winter was quite another. And when the Spaniards began to requisition food and clothing, and went so far as to chain and torture the honoured chiefs who had first brought them to this land, the indignation of the Indians could no longer be contained. Cárdenas and other officers seem to have made genuine attempts to hold their men in check and make them obey the orders to take nothing from the Indians without paying for it. But shortage of supplies was now forcing the Spaniards to live more and more off the country. Dangerous incidents began to occur. Indians from the pueblo of Arenal came to complain to Cárdenas that a soldier had repaid the services of an Indian who was holding his horse by breaking into the man's house and violating his wife. Cárdenas ordered an enquiry to be made, but the alleged culprit arrogantly denied the charges and the Indian went off vowing revenge.

Some days later frightened messengers brought news that the Indians of Arenal and neighbouring settlements were up in arms. Cárdenas hurried to investigate and found that the natives had started by slaughtering all the horses they could find and had then barricaded themselves in their pueblo. Cárdenas tried to reason with them, but his words were drowned in shouts of menace and abuse. When he returned to report to his General, Coronado summoned a council of war. The captains were unanimous that no time must be lost in bringing the Indians to obedience, if necessary by force. Cárdenas was once more despatched to make a final effort to induce them to submit peacefully. But the Indians replied only by uttering war cries and by brandishing the tails of the horses they had killed. A similar attempt to pacify the neighbouring pueblo of Moho, where the natives were also reported to be in revolt, met with no better success.

The Spaniards then prepared to crush the revolt by force, for they could not winter in the midst of a hostile and aggressive population. Cárdenas moved up with a body of sixty horse and a strong contingent of Spanish infantry and Mexican auxiliaries. After several hours hard fighting, the attackers managed to force their way on to the terraces of Arenal, and the following day they set about smoking the Indians out of their houses. A large number of prisoners were taken and sent to the Spaniards' camp where they were tied to stakes and burnt alive. Castañeda declares that the natives had given themselves up on condition that their lives would be spared, and that their execution was due to misunderstanding or treachery on the part of the Spaniards. The latter's intention was certainly to make a terrible demonstration of the fate of rebels, for Bigotes and the Turk were brought up to witness the burning. But the cruelty of the Spaniards only served to convince the Indians of Tiguex that the white men knew neither mercy nor good faith, and their resistance grew the more desperate.

The main body of the Spanish army had now come up from Cíbola, and the whole expedition, except for the small garrison under Alcaráz, left behind to guard communications at Sonora, was concentrated in Tiguex. Coronado had thus ample forces at his command, but winter was setting in and heavy falls of snow hampered operations. The messengers sent to demand the submission of the other pueblos found them deserted. Despite the cruel weather, the inhabitants had abandoned their homes rather than await the coming of the Spaniards. Only Moho, one of the largest and most impregnable of the pueblos, was confident that it could hold out. The place had been converted into a temporary capital and stronghold for the whole region. Attempts to storm the walls were beaten off with heavy loss, and the Spaniards were forced to lay regular siege in the hope of reducing the defenders by thirst. For some weeks the Indians managed to meet their needs by melting the snow and digging wells inside the pueblo. But thirst at last compelled the warriors to drive out their women and children into the arms of the besiegers, and then to attempt a break-out in force themselves. Some reached the banks of the Río Grande, where many perished in the icy water or under the spears of the Spanish horsemen. Moho was taken and active resistance finally stamped out. But the twelve towns of Tiguex were never reoccupied by their inhabitants while the Spaniards remained in the land.

Meanwhile the irrepressible Turk had kept expectations high by ever more fantastic tales of Quivira. The Spaniards seemed as if hypnotized by his words, and not a few believed that he was endowed with supernatural powers. Casteñeda declares that 'a Spaniard called Cervantes, who had charge of him during the siege, solemnly swore that he had seen the Turk talking with the devil in a pitcher of water, and that while he had him under lock so that no one could speak to him, the Turk had asked what Christians had been killed by the people of Tiguex. He said nobody had been killed, and then the Turk answered; "You are lying; five Christians are dead, including a Captain." And as Cervantes knew that he told the truth, he admitted it so as to find out who had told him about it, and the Turk said he knew it all by himself, and that he did not need to have anyone tell him in order to know it. And it was on account of this that he watched him and saw him speaking to the devil in a pitcher, as I have said.'[1]

Though not all the Spaniards were as credulous as Cervantes, the hold which the Turk maintained over the minds of Coronado and many of his officers was extra-

[1] Hodge & Lewis, op. cit., p. 328.

ordinary. Not a trace had been found of the golden bracelet which the Turk claimed would prove the truth of everything he said. And yet, as soon as the spring came round, the Spaniards made ready to march wherever he would guide them, bracelet or no bracelet. A belated attempt was made, it is true, to conciliate Bigotes and the old chief, for Pecos lay on the route to Quivira, and now that the friendship of the Tiguex Indians had been lost, it was essential that the large pueblo commanding the gateway to the plains should at least not prove openly hostile. So first the old chief, and then Bigotes himself, were restored to their people.

For four days the army marched on beyond Pecos, along the river of the same name, then halted for another four while a bridge was built to span it. The expedition had snowballed into almost a mass migration. Castañeda tells us that there were as many as a thousand horses, a flock of five thousand sheep, five hundred cattle, and more than one thousand five hundred people including the Indians from Mexico and the hostages taken along from Tiguex. Perhaps the chronicler exaggerates, but it must certainly have been a great and varied host which crossed the river, swollen with the melted snows, and made its way eastward across the plateau until, as Coronado wrote to the King, 'I reached some plains, so vast that I did not find their limit anywhere I went, although I travelled over them for 300 leagues.' Later travellers were to call this vast region the Llano Estacado, the Staked (or more accurately, the Stockaded or Palisaded) Plains, from the distant rim of mountain crests which fenced around the otherwise featureless prairie.

Soon the Spaniards came upon the vast buffalo herds, and following them, a breed of men who lived off the beasts – men 'called Querechos, who travel around with these cows, who do not plant, and who eat the raw flesh and drink the blood of the cows they kill, then tan the skin of the cows, with which all folk dress themselves. They have little field

Indians advancing in order of battle.

An Indian Pueblo.

tents made of the hides of the cows, all tanned and greased, very well made, in which they travel around near the cows, moving with these. They have dogs which they load and which carry their tents and poles and belongings."[1] These Indians came out to stare, but they were neither frightened nor hostile. Castañeda noted that they were intelligent, and were so adept in the use of sign language, that there was no need of an interpreter. The Turk, who was in the van of the immense caravan, was the first to hold converse with them – a detail of which the Spaniards only later perceived the significance.

Coronado had hitherto been following roughly the same trail as that taken by Alvarado the previous summer. To his surprise the Querechos clearly gave him to understand that they were within easy reach of a number of large settlements. These lay to the east, they declared, along the banks of a very large river, and there were so many of them that one could travel from one settlement to another for ninety days. If they went as the Querechos directed, the Spaniards would come to the first of these, which was called Haxa. Having imparted this important piece of information, the Indians struck camp and disappeared. A second band of Querechos was soon encountered and confirmed what had been said. The Spaniards were assured that they were very near Haxa. The news was welcome but puzzling. How was it that Alvarado had passed that way before, with no trace or tidings of such an important chain of settlements? The Turk had said that Quivira lay to the north-east; the Querechos repeated that it lay to the east. To add to the confusion Sopete, the other slave given to the Spaniards by Bigotes as a guide, began to protest that the Querechos and the Turk were nothing but a pack of liars, and that the expedition was being deliberately misled. But no one paid him much attention.

Coronado decided to halt while a reconnaissance party

[1] Coronado to the King, quoted in Winship, op. cit. p. 214.

went on ahead in search of Haxa. Cárdenas, who had so often proved his worth in such ventures, had broken his arm in an accident, so the command was given to Diego Lopez, an alderman of Seville. After some days, Lopez returned with no news of any settlements, but relating an astonishing and alarming adventure. It might have been dismissed as a traveller's tale, had not the loss of the horse vouch for its truth. Lopez described how he and his companions had come upon a dense herd of buffalo and 'as these fled, they trampled on one another in their haste until they came to a ravine. So many of the animals fell into this that they filled it up, and the rest went across on top of them. The men who were chasing them on horseback fell in amongst the animals without noticing where they were going. Three of the horses that fell in amongst the cows, all saddled and bridled, were lost sight of completely.'

As the reconnaissance party had not found any trace of Haxa, the expedition had no other choice but to push on in the general direction indicated by the Querechos. 'For five days I went wherever they led me,' Coronado reported, 'until we reached some plains as bereft of landmarks as if we had been swallowed up in the sea. There was not a stone, nor piece of rising ground, nor a tree, nor a shrub, nor anything to go by.' So they wandered on, the Turk confident and plausible as ever, but Sopote now openly denouncing him and declaring that he would never guide them to Quivira, and the soldiers increasingly distrustful as their strength and their food were consumed. After three weeks Coronado despatched another reconnaissance party under Rodrigo Maldonado, who sent back encouraging news. He had fallen in with some Tejas Indians, enemies of the Querechos, and had accompanied them down to a deep ravine where the Spaniards had found a settlement. The friendly Indians offered what they possessed – 'a tent as big and high as a house', and heaps of hides. The main army hurried on towards this new goal along the trail which

Maldonado had marked out with piles of buffalo chips and bones.

The Tejas Indians might well feel dismayed at the behaviour of the strangers they had welcomed to their homes. As soon as Coronado's men reached the settlement, they began to fall upon the hides and other goods which they found, each man seizing and carrying off for himself as much as he could. The Indians set up a loud lamentation. They remembered how Dorantes and Cabeza de Vaca had passed through their land, simply blessing whatever possessions the Indians offered but taking nothing for themselves. Despite their rude disillusionment, the Indians still remained friendly. Coronado learned from them that the army was in fact heading away from Quivira. Moreover, he received a very different account of what he would find if he did reach the land he was seeking. The Indians declared that it was poor in maize, and described 'the houses as being of grass and hides, and not of stone and several storeys high, as my guides alleged'. This tallied with what Sopete had been trying to tell the Spaniards. Now he deemed the moment had come to compel attention by a dramatic act. 'He threw himself down in the way,' declared Captain Jaramillo, one of Coronado's officers, 'making a sign that though we should cut off his head he would not go that way, for that was not our destination.'[1] Under fresh cross-examination, the Turk began to break down and confess that he had been deceiving them about the direction of Quivira and the quality of its inhabitants.

In the ravine where the friendly Tejas had their settlement, the Spaniards rested a while and pondered which course they should take. Amidst the desolation of the plains it seemed a pleasant oasis. In the shelter of the ravine were groves of mulberry and walnut trees, wild vines and plums, and a small river where buffalo came down to wallow. After holding a council of war, Coronado decided to push on with

[1] Jaramillo's narrative is given in Winship, op. cit. pp. 222-40.

some thirty men in an attempt to reach Quivira. The army begged to be allowed to march on with their General, but Coronado gave orders that they were to return to Tiguex and wait for him there. After resting another two weeks, and slaughtering a great number of buffalo to provide dried meat for the journey, the army regretfully started back home, leaving their General to complete the quest for Quivira.

Coronado had the best men of the expedition with him – Diego Lopez as his second in command, Maldonado, Alvarado, Jaramillo, Friar Juan de Padilla, and others. Sopete was now promoted to chief guide, but the Turk was also taken along in chains, for Coronado could not rid himself of the conviction that he might after all prove useful. The party travelled light, living off the herds in the way they had learned from the Indians. A few Tejas accompanied him, guiding the Spaniards along the buffalo trails which led nearly due north along the great escarpment towards the basin of the Arkansas River. After nearly a month's march, they reached this stream, which Sopete joyfully declared he recognized, and after crossing it by a ford used by the buffalo, followed its northern bank. The country was rolling and fertile. The Indians whom they encountered made off in fear, until Sopete called out to them in their own tongue, when they came peacefully and stared at the strangers and at the still stranger beasts they rode. The Spaniards had reached the borders of Quivira. This land is known today as Kansas, and the river as the Arkansas. No more than three hundred miles downstream, a short distance in the immensity of the plains, de Soto's expedition had also reached the Arkansas. But neither band knew about the other, and from this point their routes and destinies once more diverged.

Was Coronado now on the threshold of a rich and fertile land – clearly not so fabulous in its wealth of gold and silver as the Turk made out, but a great empire neverthe-

less? Somehow – perhaps through some quirk of mistrans-
lation or misapprehension – the Spaniards had gained the
impression that the land they had come to was ruled by
a Christian lord. Perhaps there lingered in their minds some
memory of the ancient myth of the Seven Cities. The myth
which had first hovered over the elusive isles of Antillia and
then over the stone and adobe walls of Cíbola, now seemed
to have found a new incarnation in Quivira and in this
Prester John of the prairies. Or perhaps there had reached
them some rumour, borne along the mysterious grape-vine
of native communication, of the presence of white men
who had crossed the Mississippi bent on the same quest as
themselves – their rivals, the men of de Soto. Or it might be
that some survivor of the Narváez expedition, long since
deemed dead, had founded a secret kingdom of his own in
Quivira, or in the even more distant land of Harahey.
However the belief arose, it was real enough, as we learn
from the curious detail which Jaramillo records; 'The
General wrote a letter here to the Governor of Harahey
and Quivira, having understood that he was a Christian from
the lost army of Florida, because of what the Indians had
said of their manner of Government and their general
character had made us believe this.' Into whose hands this
strange missive was delivered, and what its recipients made
of it, we do not know. The Indians went off to their own
settlements, and the Spaniards followed expectantly.

Quivira proved to be an exceptionally beautiful land of
green meadows watered by streams flowing into the broad
Arkansas, and its inhabitants members of the tall, handsome,
dark-skinned Wichita tribe. Their muscular, tattooed
bodies, and the challenging arrogance of the topknots in
which they wore their hair proclaimed them to be warlike.
They received the Spaniards hospitably, for the presence
of Sopete gave them the assurance that the strangers came
in peace. But their primitive manner of life was a bitter
disappointment to Coronado. 'As barbarous as all those

whom I have seen and passed before this,' he wrote to the King. 'They have no cloaks, nor cotton from which to make them, but use the skins of the cattle which they kill.' They lived in straw-thatched huts, grouped in a couple of dozen settlements, which, he adds, in dutiful rather than enthusiastic tones, 'have given their obedience to Your Majesty and placed themselves under your protection'.

Coronado was at length informed that the lord of Quivira was ready to receive the strangers. The Spaniards had heard a grandiose and detailed description of this potentate from the Turk, who declared that his name was Tatarrax.[1] He was the dignified prince, grey-haired and bearded, who took his siesta under a tree lulled by the jingling of golden bells dangling from its boughs, and he would go sailing in a boat whose prow was a great golden eagle. Whether this Tatarrax was to be identical with the Christian ruler to whom the General had written no one quite knew. Perhaps so, for the Turk had also described Tatarrax as 'reading from a book of hours, and worshipping a woman, Queen of Heaven'. When the mighty prince at length appeared before them, the Spaniards found him to be a tall savage whose chief mark of distinction was a copper ornament which he wore round his neck. This he graciously presented, in sign of friendship, to the General, who had it sent on to the Viceroy. Of other treasure there was no trace, except for a piece of gold whose origin puzzled the Spaniards until Coronado discovered it had in fact belonged to someone in his own suite.

The meeting with Tatarrax set the seal on the Spaniards' disillusionment. It also cured them of the lingering belief that there might be some basis for the Turk's grandiloquent assertions. Moreover, though disgraced, manacled, and kept in the background, he was still in a position to do them serious harm. He had been discovered in secret converse with the Indians of Quivira, inciting them to make a surprise

[1] The Wichita term for a chief or headman.

attack on the Spaniards and start by slaughtering their horses. Reluctantly, for Coronado seems to have had a liking for him, the General gave his consent that the Turk should be silenced once and for all. The prisoner was summoned to the tent of Diego Lopez and questioned for the last time. He no longer denied that he had lied and misled them, but he blamed it all on Bigotes, who he alleged had made him promise to lead the army astray in the pathless plains so that their provisions might run out, their horses die, and the white men never return to plague the Indians of Pecos and Tiguex. Was the Turk telling the truth, or was he trying, in one last spate of perjury, to turn the Spaniards against his master, as he had so successfully done before? The Turk now played his last card. He swore that he had really wanted the Spaniards to come to Quivira because he had a wife living there whom he wished to see; the real land of marvels, where the Spaniards would find the treasures he had told them about, was further off – in Harahey, his true home. But the Turk's words had lost their power to bewitch; besides, from questioning the natives, the Spaniards had learned that Harahey was much the same size and type of place as Quivira, save that there the Indians lived in houses made of hides.[1] So the Turk was no longer believed, a rope was slipped round his neck and the garrote twisted. He was buried in secret by Lopez's tent, to the immense satisfaction of his enemy Sopete. Only Coronado grieved, for with the Turk were buried the last of the General's golden hopes.

After three weeks spent in exploring Quivira and collecting reports of the neighbouring lands, Coronado summoned his captains to council. 'It seemed to everyone,' writes Jaramillo, 'that since the winter would soon be at hand – for if I remember rightly it was past the middle of August –

[1] It is now thought that Harahey was a settlement of Pawnee Indians in Nebraska.

and since there were so few of us to establish winter quarters, and because of the scantiness of our provisions, we decided with one accord that His Lordship should turn back.' But, added the captain, 'at the beginning of the summer we should return to that land to explore and cultivate it'. The faithful Sopete was presented with a handsome present and allowed to remain with his people. After collecting supplies of maize and erecting crosses with an inscription recording that Vasquez de Coronado had reached that spot, the Spaniards prepared to leave Quivira.[1] Six Quivira Indians accompanied them back to Pecos. The General was anxious to reach it as soon as possible and the guides knew of a more direct route; up the Arkansas, then veering to the south-west and striking what later generations would know as the Santa Fé trail between New Mexico and St Louis.

On rejoining the main body of the army, Coronado found that there had, as he feared, been clashes between the Spaniards and the followers of Bigotes. Whether there was any truth in the Turk's charges that Bigotes had hatched a plot to destroy the Spaniards, Coronado never discovered. Soon after his arrival the whole army evacuated Pecos without further incident and spent an uncomfortable winter in Tiguex. In the months which followed, the men, who were quartered once again in Alcanfor, found little to do and less to eat. A limited supply of maize could still be had from neighbouring pueblos, and there were the remnants of the sheep from Mexico and the jerked buffalo meat from the Great Plains. But the men grew dispirited and quarrelsome, grumbled that the officers were distributing the rations unfairly, and blamed them for not having led the army on to Quivira and the rich lands promised by the Turk. Again the Turk! Not even the grave could silence him, for he spoke to the Spaniards with the voice of their

---

[1] Recent research has established that Coronado penetrated as far into Kansas as the village of Lindsberg in MacPherson County.

own unquenchable desires. And like a faint echo of his words, there could now be heard the tales of another slave, a young Wichita Indian called Xabe, who declared to all and sundry that there *was* gold in Quivira, though not in such abundance as the Turk had claimed, and that if the Spaniards had not found it they could not have looked hard enough. Many who had not been to Quivira lent a ready ear to Xabe's assertions. Coronado, to placate them and raise morale through hope of better things to come, and because it was his intention to return and possibly found a settlement there, promised he would lead the army to Quivira when spring came round.

But fate willed it otherwise. While out riding one day, Coronado fell from his horse and received serious injuries from which his recovery was slow and uncertain. After the accident his resolution began to waver. Castañeda tells us that while the General lay on his sick-bed, his mind became obsessed with superstitious memories of how a soothsayer had once foretold of him that 'he would become a powerful lord in distant lands and that he would have a fall from which he would never manage to recover. This expectation of death,' Castañeda concludes, 'made him desire to return and die where he had a wife and children.'

Coronado's accident was more than a personal misfortune; it marked the end of the whole expedition. A mood of depression began to spread throughout the entire army. Those whose minds were most set on giving up the campaign took advantage of the General's state to 'set the soldiers talking in little knots and gatherings about going back to New Spain, and induced them to hold consultations about it, and had them send petitions to the General, signed by the soldiers, through their ensigns, asking for this.' Coronado at first made a show of resistance, but when the officers openly voiced the same opinion as the men and added their signatures to the petitions, the General concurred and announced that the expedition would return to

Mexico. A few seem to have quickly regretted their action and attempted to withdraw their signatures. But the sick General guarded his papers well, and likewise rejected various compromise proposals to the effect that a part of the army only should return to Mexico, whilst the rest remained to garrison Tiguex. His mind was now as firmly set on withdrawal as it once had been on pressing forward. Only one or two friars were allowed to remain behind to spread the Gospel among the natives. Early in April 1542, after more than two years' absence from Mexico, Coronado's army began the long trek homewards.

CHAPTER XI

Epilogue

Coronado had failed. The Seven Cities of Cíbola had been found and conquered; strange, remote lands had been discovered and explored and their inhabitants brought at least to a nominal allegiance to the Crown; the General had led his army back without serious loss; more remarkable still, less than thirty of the hundreds of Mexican auxiliaries who accompanied him had perished. But the Spaniards had returned with empty hands. Had not Columbus himself declared that 'Gold is most excellent; of gold is treasure made; with gold the man who possesses it does all that he desires in the world and may even send souls to Paradise'? Without gold, then, a conquest was barren. In the eyes of his contemporaries, Coronado's expedition had proved a fiasco.

Castañeda tells us that the General was coldly received by the Viceroy when he reached Mexico. Mendoza must have been as keenly disappointed as was his former favourite at the ill success of the expedition. But there was no open disgrace. The Crown ordered a searching enquiry to be made into Coronado's conduct of the campaign. If no treasure trove was there to find, the General could hardly be blamed for failing to return with it, but the prosecution could at least allege that through the fighting in Tiguex and the decision not to found any settlement 'the royal patrimony was denied the opportunity of securing more than 500,000 ducats in gold, silver, and other things'. Coronado was finally cleared of the charges of incompetence and ill-treatment of the natives and he retained his governorship of New Galicia for a couple of years and held a number of lesser offices thereafter. But he paid dearly in health and fortune for the failure of his expedition. 'Francisco Vasquez has come back home, where he is more fit to be governed in it than to govern outside of it,' wrote the investigating judge. 'He is lacking in many of his former fine qualities and is not the same man he was when Your Majesty appointed him to the Governorship. They say this change was caused by the fall from his horse which he suffered in the exploration and pacification of Tierra Nueva.' The conqueror of Cíbola was never called upon again to play a major part in the affairs of the New World. He died, still a relatively young man, twelve years after the return of his expedition.

The fate of the other protagonists can be briefly told. Friar Marcos, whose fantasies had raised expectations to such a feverish height, passed the remainder of his life in the seclusion of Mexican monasteries. His exertions had left him a cripple, and apart from a brief note that the Bishop had graciously granted him a monthly ration of wine in alleviation of his ills, the friar's name vanishes from the records. Cárdenas, invalided home with a broken arm and hopes of a family inheritance, faced many years of trial and imprisonment on charges similar to those of his chief before he was allowed to live out the rest of his days in peace. Alvarado, the first explorer of the plains and the baiter of Bigotes, appears never to have been called to account. Of the friars who chose to remain and spread the faith in the new lands, little is known except that one escaped to bring back news of the other's death. Juan de Padilla, the fighting friar, found a martyr's crown in Quivira.

As far as the rank and file of the army is concerned, history has not much to say beyond what Castañeda, one of their number, tells us. So long as we possess a thing, the old soldier philosophically reflects, we take it for granted, 'and the longer we continue to have it, the less we value it. But once we lose it, and miss the advantage of it, we have a great pain in the heart, and we are all the time imagining and trying to find ways and means of getting it back again. This, it seems to me, is what happened to all or most of those who went on the expedition which, in the year 1540 of Our Saviour Jesus Christ, Francisco Vasquez de Coronado led in search of the Seven Cities. Granted that they did not find the riches of which they had been told, they found a place in which to search for them, and the beginning of a good country to settle in, from where they could go on further. Since they returned from the country which they conquered and abandoned, time has given them a chance to understand the direction and locality in which they were, and the borders of the good country they had in their hands, and their hearts weep for having lost so favourable an opportunity.'

The Inca Garcilaso says that those who survived the great misfortunes of de Soto's expedition were tormented by similar regrets the moment they returned to the safety of the first Spanish settlements around the Pánuco River. 'And now, as they compared certain things with others, the glory of the many fine provinces they had discovered increased . . . they recalled the fertility and abundance of all these places, their natural fitness for bearing the seeds, grains, and vegetables that they could bring to them from Spain, and the advantage offered in their pasture lands, woods, and rivers for raising and multiplying whatever livestock they might wish to breed. Finally, they remembered the great wealth of pearls and seed pearls they had scorned, and the splendours in which they had seen themselves, for each man of them had fancied himself as the lord of a great province. And as they compared those riches and noble estates with these present miseries and paucities, some discussed their visions and melancholy thoughts with others, and with most sorrowful hearts and self-pity remarked; "Could we not have lived in Florida as these Spaniards are living in Pánuco? Were not the lands we left better than those where we are

at present? . . . Were it not better to have died there, than
to live here?"'

But though the veterans of the de Soto and Coronado
expeditions might soon forget their past sufferings and
declare themselves ready, with the irrepressible optimism
of defrauded adventurers, to try their luck again, the
authorities were more cautious. Expeditions were costly
affairs, and the two latest, which had been expected to pay
for themselves many times over, had in fact only proved
the ruin of their sponsors. Mendoza, his natural prudence
deepened by disappointment, anxiously deliberated whether
any further attempt to open up the lands to the north and
north-east of New Spain would be justified, and if so, where
a settlement should be attempted – in Cíbola and Quivira
or on the coast of Florida and its vast hinterland? Quivira at
first seemed the most promising, and plans were considered
for reaching it by routes more direct than the roundabout
coastal trail followed by Friar Marcos and Coronado. But
the project came to nought, and Mendoza was transferred
to the Viceroyalty of Peru and to other cares and hopes.
Under his successor, Luís de Velasco, plans for colonization
were revived. The objective this time was Florida and the
north coast of the Gulf of Mexico. In 1559, six of de Soto's
former officers, under the command of Tristan de Luna y
Arellano, who had led the main body of Coronado's army on
the march to Cíbola, set sail with thirteen ships and a motley
company of colonists, soldiers, women, children, servants
and negro slaves. Settlement rather than conquest was the
aim, but the venture was incompetently handled and the
colonists' attempts to establish themselves at various points
along the coast all met with failure, and the expedition withdrew in discouragement to Mexico.

Meanwhile, experiments of a different sort were being
made to turn the discoveries of the early explorers to
account. If the soldiers and the colonists had failed, could
not the missionaries be given their chance? The Crown,

moved by the pious eloquence of Bartolomé de las Casas, was sympathetic. A Dominican friar called Luís Cancer, who had achieved some success amongst the Indians of Mexico, was permitted to take four other monks with him and continue his labours in Florida. With tragic misjudgment the missionaries chose to land somewhere in the region of Tampa Bay where the natives had already been driven into implacable opposition to the white men. Friar Luís and two of his companions were martyred almost as soon as they had landed, and the rest of his party were driven off. Seventeen years later a group of Jesuit missionaries landed in Florida. They too were either killed or forced to flee. Eight more Jesuits followed a couple of years later, only to meet with similar fate. The natural savagery of the Florida Indians, and the legacy of Narváez and de Soto, rendered them the least promising of proselytes.

So long as these vast and potentially prosperous lands remained half known and unheld, they represented a standing temptation to other European powers whose appetite for overseas adventure and a share in the spoils of the New World was growing voraciously. The idea of starting a colony somewhere on the east coast of Florida, which might also serve as a base for attacking the Spanish treasure fleet as it sailed homewards along the Bahamas passage, appealed with special force to the French Huguenots. Coligny commissioned Jean Ribault and René Laudonnière to reconnoitre. They reported that the country seemed suitable for colonization and the natives friendly. A fortified settlement was accordingly founded near the mouth of the St John's River, not far from where Jacksonville stands today. The French had no doubt studied the important collection of Spanish voyages and exploration published in Venice by Ramusio, which included Friar Marcos' account of the splendours of Cíbola. The colonists eagerly questioned the natives as to the whereabouts of Cíbola, and were delighted to understand from them that it lay no more than twenty days' journey inland. The mirage of the Seven Cities beckoned once again!

News that the French Huguenots had established themselves in Florida caused alarm and indignation in the Spanish Court. Pedro Menéndez de Avilés, Spain's best admiral, was despatched with orders to suppress the colony forthwith, and to secure Florida for Spain once and for all. Avilés carried out his task with merciless thoroughness. In 1565, the French garrison was overpowered and massacred, the base destroyed. Not far off, Avilés then founded his own settlement of St Augustine. It was not an easy outpost to maintain. Hardship and loneliness led to frequent desertions amongst the garrison. But somehow it survived to become the first of Spain's settlements in Florida.

Avilés was eager to remain in Florida to govern the colony which he had founded, but his master recalled him to take charge of the preparations for assembling an armada against England. 'Having told His Majesty of my unhappiness at being away from Florida,' he wrote to his nephew and heir, on whom he laid the obligation of living in the colony for at least ten years, 'he has graciously told me that whenever it becomes possible he will very willingly permit me to return there. And I hope – God willing – that he will do so in the spring, because I believe that without a doubt the Flanders matter will be settled this winter; and that this being the case I will be free to go directly to Florida, never to leave thence as long as I live; for my desires and happiness consist of none other than that. May Our Lord do as He is able and as He sees fit.' God saw fit that the Admiral should die before he could see his colony again, for 'the Flanders matter' was far from being settled that winter. But, more fortunate than the many captains who had sought fame and fortune in Florida, Menéndez de Avilés will be remembered as the Governor whose colony at last made good.

The effective colonization of Cíbola and Quivira did not

A Pueblo village, New Mexico.

The Pueblo of Walpi, Arizona,

follow until later. Individual Spaniards occasionally revisited the scenes of Coronado's adventures, but it was not until 1595 that Pueblo Land was occupied afresh and settled by Spaniards under the command of Juan de Oñate. Though shaken nearly a century later by the desperate Taos Indian revolt of 1680, which lasted for a dozen years and left many pueblos deserted, Cíbola and Quivira remained frontier provinces of the far-flung empire of Spain until their destinies were merged at last into that of the United States of America.

Myth dies slowly. Sooner than succumb beneath the sharp impact of reality, it tends to assume new forms and live on. Mirage shifts and refashions as the seeker advances. Visions are not subject to the laws of time, place, or logic, nor to the lessons of experience. For many years after Coronado had proved that the gold and jem-encrusted cities of his desires were nothing more than wretched Indian pueblos, the cartographers persisted in marking the Seven Cities on their maps. A map drawn by Johannes Martines of Messina about 1578,[1] thirty-eight years after Coronado had learnt the discouraging truth, still gives exuberant form to the fantasy. A glorious Cíbola is shown, each of its seven component cities marked with domes, towers, and fluttering banners. A later generation of French settlers, as we have seen, eagerly asked for news of Cíbola and was given it with obliging insouciance by the natives. A ripple of the excitement which had once stirred New Spain at length reached England, and in the 'Relation of Henry Hawks, merchant, who lived for five years in Nova Hispania' and committed his wisdom to paper at the request of Richard Hakluyt in 1572, we find memories of Cabeza de Vaca, Hernán de Soto, Friar Marcos and Coronado, all merged together in dream-like yet alluring inconsequence:

'There is a great number of beasts or kine in the country

[1] See front endpaper.

of Cíbola, which were never before brought thither by the
Spanyards, but breed naturally in that country. They are
like unto our oxen, saving that they have long haire like a
lion, and short hornes, and they have upon their shoulders
a bunch like a camell, which is higher than the rest of the
body. They are marvellously wild and swift in running.
They call them the beasts or kine of Cíbola. This Cíbola
is a city which the Spaniards found now of late, without
any people in the same, goodly buildings, faire chimneys,
windowes made of stone and timber excellently wrought,
faire welles with wheeles to draw their water, and a place
where they had buried their dead people, with many faire
stones upon the graves. And the Captain would not suffer
his souldiers to break up any part of these graves, saying, he
would come another time to do it. They asked certain
people which they met, whither the people of this city
were gone, and they made answere, they were gone downe
a river, which was thereby, very great, and there had builded
a city which was more for their commodity. This Captain,
lacking things necessary for himself and his men, was faine
to return back againe, without finding any treasure according to his expectation; neither found they but five people,
although they found beaten wayes, which had been much
haunted and frequented. The Captain at his coming backe
againe had a great checke of the governor, because he had
not gone forwards and seen the end of that river.'

Is this a real or a dream world of which Henry Hawks,
merchant, speaks? Had the Spaniards truly laid bare all the
secrets of the land explored by their captains? The narrator
can scarcely bring himself to believe it. 'The Spanyards
have notice of Seven Cities,' he declares, 'which old men
of the Indians show them should lie towards the North-east
from Mexico. They have used and use daily much diligence
in seeking of them, but they cannot find any one of them.
They say that the witchcraft of the Indians is such, that
when they come by these townes' they cast a mist upon

them, so that they cannot see them.' So the Seven Cities might very well still exist, even though the Spaniards had not yet managed to find them. And where they had failed, others might take up the quest. Spain's heroic age of discovery, conquest, and colonization is drawing to an end; England's day is dawning. The great Elizabethans are setting forth on their adventures. They too will go in quest of rich lands and fabulous cities. For some of the noblest and most ardent spirits amongst them, Cíbola will still weave its magic spell, promising fame and fortune, but luring on to disaster. Only the name will be changed. Men will know the goal of their desires as El Dorado.

The centuries pass, and then all at once, when men had long ceased from the quest and lost the very memory of the legend, the mists are blown aside to reveal – if not the Seven Cities, the treasure which had made men so eager to discover them.

In January 1848, more than three hundred years after Coronado had returned from his great trek with empty hands, a young New Jersey wagon builder named James Wilson Marshall, who was working on a saw-mill in a fork of the American River near Coloma, picked out of the water a small piece of shining metal half the size of a pea. Gold had at last been found – not in Cíbola, Quivira, or Harahey, but in California, the 'island' which an ancient romance of chivalry had declared was near the Terrestrial Paradise and inhabited by black women wielding arms of gold. Now gold was revealed in a profusion more lavish than the visions of Friar Marcos or the fantasies of the Turk. Marshall's discovery launched the greatest gold-rush in history. Where gold was to be found, people flocked in thousands and cities began to arise – not seven, but many times that number, the great cities of California where men and women still come in pursuit of fame and fortune, and which have in turn become a potent legend in our own days.

Table of Events

1540 The Viceroy sends an expedition under Francisco Vasquez de Coronado, who conquers the Seven Cities.

1541 Coronado occupies Tiguex and pushes on over the Great Plains to Quivira.

1542 Coronado suffers an accident and returns to Mexico. De Soto dies and is buried in the Mississippi.

1543 Survivors of the de Soto expedition reach Mexico.

1549 Friar Luís Cancer and other monks attempt to start a mission in Florida but are martyred.

1559 Unsuccessful attempts to colonize Florida by Tristan de Luna y Arellano.

1565 Menéndez de Avilés destroys a French outpost in Florida and founds the first permanent settlement.

1595 Cíbola and Quivira colonized under Juan de Oñate.

Bibliography

The main sources for any study of the Spanish expeditions to Florida and Cíbola are to be found in the reports, narratives, and despatches of those who themselves played some part in those ventures. The first substantial narrative is the *Relación* of Alvar Nuñez Cabeza de Vaca, an officer who was one of the four survivors of Narváez's ill-fated expedition to Florida. His narrative was first published at Zamora in 1542, an English version being printed by Samual Purchas in his *Pilgrimes* in 1613 (Cap. i, lib. viii, Part iv).

The fullest first-hand account of de Soto's expedition is given by an anonymous Portuguese soldier generally referred to as the Gentleman of Elvas. This was first published in Portugal in 1557 and was translated into English and published by Hakluyt in 1609 under the title *Virginia richly valued by the Description of the Mainland of Florida*. Ranjel, de Soto's secretary, has left a narrative which is reproduced in Oviedo's *Historia General de las Indias* (Seville, 1547), and another short account was drawn up by Biedma, the Factor of the expedition. The Inca Garcilaso de la Vega, the well-known historian of the conquest of Peru, also composed a history of the de Soto expedition, generally known as *La Florida del Inca*, with the object of extolling the exploits both of the Spanish and the Indian races. He took no part in the expedition himself, but drew on the written narratives of two soldiers who served in it, Alonso de Camona and Juan Coles, and on the reminiscences of his friend Gonzalo Silvestre. Due allowance made for the author's tendency to idealize all concerned, specially the natives, and to concoct courtly speeches, Garcilaso's history is more trustworthy in its main lines, and in its vivid use of detail, than some historians have been prepared to admit.

The chief source for the history of Coronado's expedition is the somewhat crusty but honest narrative of Pedro de Castañeda, who served as a soldier under him. The chief protagonists in the expedition have left some documentation, unfortunately incomplete, which includes the following; Friar Marcos's report on his own expedition of 1539, Coronado's letter to Viceroy Mendoza, written shortly after he had taken possession of the first of the Seven Cities, the Viceroy's despatch to the King reporting the start of Coronado's expedition, Coronado's letter to the King, dated 20 October, 1541, from Tiguex, after the return of his expedition from Quivira, a short report by Captain Jaramillo, and other brief anonymous reports. The testimony given by Coronado and other officers after his expedition returned to Mexico is also extant.

The works chiefly consulted in the preparation of this book have been:

Anghiera, Pietro Martire d': *De Orbe Novo*; the Eight Decades of Peter Martyr, translated by F. A. MacNutt, N.Y. and London, 1912. Spanish translation by Torres Asensio, ed. Luís A. Arocena, Buenos Aires, 1944.

Babcock, William H.: *Legendary Islands of the Atlantic*, N.Y., 1922.

Bandelier, A. F.: *Contributions to the History of the South-Western Portion of the United States*, Archaeological Society of America (American Series) Vol. V, Cambridge, Mass., 1890.

Barrientos, Bartolomé: *Vida y hechos de Pedro Menéndez de Avilés*, in *Dos Antiguas Relaciones de la Florida*, Mexico, 1902.

Biedma, Luis Hernandez de: *Relación del suceso de la jornada que hizo Hernando de Soto*, in *Colección de Documentos inéditos . . . de India y Oceania*, Madrid,

1864-84. English translation by Bourne, op. cit.

Bishop, Morris: *The Odyssey of Cabeza de Vaca*, N.Y. and London, 1933.

Bourne, Edward Gaylord (Ed.): *Narratives of the Career of Hernando de Soto*, tr. by Buckingham Smith, N.Y., 1904.

Cabeza de Vaca, Alvar Nuñez de: *Relación de los Naufragios*, ed. M. Serrano y Sanz, Madrid, 1906. *The Narrative of*, Eng. translation by Buckingham Smith, ed. F. W. Hodge, in *Spanish Explorers of the Southern United States*, N.Y., 1907.

Castañeda, Pedro de: *Narrative of the Expedition to Cíbola*, Eng. translation by G. P. Winship from manuscript now in N.Y. Public Library, in *The Journey of Coronado*, N.Y., 1922, and *Spanish Explorers in the Southern United States*, ed. F. W. Hodge, N.Y., 1907.

Collis, Maurice: *Cortés and Montezuma*, London, 1954.

Columbus, Christopher: *The Journal*, and *Letter announcing the results of his First Voyage*, tr. Cecil Jane, ed. Vigneras, London, 1960.

Columbus, Fernando: *The Life of the Admiral Christopher Columbus, by his son*, tr. and ed. by B. Keen, London, 1960.

Coronado, Francisco Vasquez de: *Carta al Emperador*, 20 October, 1541, in *Colección de Documentos Inéditos . . . de Indias*, Vol. 3, Eng. tr. in Hammond and Rey, and in Winship, op. cit. *Letter to the Viceroy*, 3 August, 1940, Eng. tr. in Hammond and Rey and in Winship, op. cit.

Cortés, Hernán: *Cartas y Relaciones*, ed. Pascual de Guayangos, Paris, 1866. Eng. tr. by F. A. MacNutt, N.Y. and London, 1908, two vols.

Cushing, F. H.: *Zuñi Folk Tales*, N.Y., 1901.

Day, A. Grove: *Coronado's Quest*, Cambridge, 1941.

DeVoto, B.: *Westward the Course of Empire* (London, 1954).

Escalante, Fontaneda: *Memoria de las Cosas y costa y indios de la Florida, 1575,* in *Colección de Documentos inéditos . . . de America,* vol. 5. Eng. tr. by Buckingham Smith, Miami, Florida, 1944.

Elvas, Hidalgo de: *Relaçao Verdadeira,* ed. Gavazzo Perry Vidal, Lisbon, 1940. Spanish tr. by Muñoz de San Pedro, *Colección Austral,* Madrid, 1952. Eng. tr. by Buckingham Smith, ed. T. H. Lewis, in *Spanish Explorers in the Southern United States,* ed. F. W. Hodge, 1907.

García Icazbalceta, Joaquín de: *Colección de Documentos inéditos para la historia de Mexico,* 1858, 1866 (2 vols.).

Garcilaso de la Vega, el Inca: *La Florida del Inca,* Lisbon, 1605. Eng. tr. by J. G. and J. J. Varner, Austin (Texas) and Edinburgh, 1951.

Hakluyt, Richard: *The Principal Navigations, Voyages, Traffiques and Discoveries of the English Nation.* Various editions.

Hammond, George P. and Agapito Rey: *Narratives of the Coronado Expedition,* Albuquerque, 1940.

Hellenbeck, Cleve: *The Journey and Route of Alvar Nuñez Cabeza de Vaca,* Glendale (California), 1940.

Herrera, Antonio de: *Historia General de los hechos de los Castellanos,* Madrid, 1601-1615. Reprinted, Asunción and Buenos Aires, 1944-47, 10 vols.

Hodge, F.W., and Lewis, T. H.: *Spanish Explorers in the Southern United States, 1528-43,* N.Y., 1907.

Jaramillo, Juan: *Relación . . . de Cíbola,* Eng. tr. in Winship, op. cit.

Kirkpatrick, F. A.: *The Spanish Conquistadores,* London, 1946.

Marcos de Nizza: *Relación del descubrimiento de las Siete Ciudades,* in *Colección de Documentos Inéditos . . . de Indias,* Vol. 3. Eng. tr. in Bandelier, and in Hammond and Rey, op. cit.

Mendoza, Antonio de: *Carta a la Emperatriz,* 11 February, 1537 (regarding Cabeza de Vaca and Dorantes) in

Colección de documentos inéditos . . . de America, Vol. 14.

Carta al Emperador, 17 April, 1540 (regarding Coronado's expedition) in *Colección de Documentos inéditos . . . de Indias,* Vol. 2. Eng. tr. in Winship and in Hammond and Rey, op. cit.

Morrison, S. E.: *Christopher Columbus, Admiral of the Ocean Sea,* 2 vols., Boston, 1942.

Oviedo y Valdés, Gonzalo Fernandez de: *Historia General de las Indias,* Seville, 1535; reprinted, Madrid, 1851.

Prescott, W. H.: *History of Ferdinand and Isabella,* New York, 1838. *History of the Conquest of Mexico,* New York, 1843.

Priestley, H. L.: *The Luna Papers: Documents relating to the Expedition of Don Tristan de Luna y Arellano for the Conquest of Florida in 1559-61,* Florida, 1928.

Ranjel, Rodrigo: *Journal of de Soto's Expedition,* reproduced in Oviedo, op. cit. Eng. tr. in Bourne, op. cit.

Ruidias y Caravia, Eugenio: *La Florida, su conquista y colonización por Pedro Menéndez de Avilés,* Madrid, 1893, 12 vols.

Sauer, Carl O.: *The Road to Cíbola,* Berkeley, 1932.

Stevenson, M. C.: *The Zuñi Indians; their mythology, esoteric fraternities and ceremonies,* U.S. Bureau of American Ethnology, Washington, 1904.

Swanton, John R.: *The Indians of the Southern United States,* U.S. Bureau of American Ethnology, Washington, 1946.

Wagner, H. R.: *California Voyages, 1539-41,* San Francisco, 1925.
The Spanish Southwest, 1542-1794, an annotated bibliography, Albuquerque, 1937, 2 vols.

Winship, G. P.: *The Coronado Expedition, 1540-42,* U.S. Bureau of American Ethnology, Washington, 1896.
The Journey of Coronado, 1540-42, New York, 1922.

NOTE ON THE ILLUSTRATIONS

Many of the illustrations for this book are reproduced from the work of Theodore de Bry (1528-98), a distinguished German engraver and acquaintance of Richard Hakluyt. He is particularly known for his great collection of travel narratives entitled *Collectiones Peregrinationum in Indiam Orientalem et Indiam Occidentalem*, which was published in twenty-five parts between 1590 and 1634, de Bry's son continuing the work after his death.

The drawing of the buffalo on page 67 is taken from Andre Thevet's *Les Singvlaritez de la France Antartiqve*, Paris, 1558.

Index

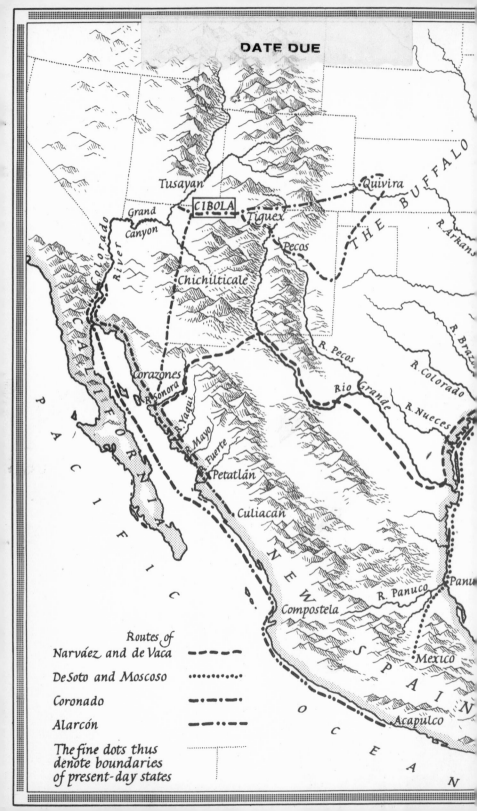

DATE DUE

PACIFIC OCEAN

THE BUFFALO

CALIFORNIA

NEW SPAIN

Tusayan

CIBOLA

Tiguex

Quivira

Grand Canyon

Pecos

Colorado River

Chichilticale

R. Arkansas

Corazones

Sonora

Yaqui

R. Mayo

Fuerte

Petatlán

Culiacán

R. Pecos

Rio Grande

R. Brazos

R. Colorado

R. Nueces

Compostela

R. Panuco

Panu

Mexico

Acapulco

Routes of
Narváez and de Vaca   — — —

De Soto and Moscoso   ············

Coronado   —·—·—·—

Alarcón   —··—··—

The fine dots thus
denote boundaries
of present-day states